Bootstrap 5 Foundations

https://www.foremanlearning.com

Written by Daniel Foreman

Revision 2

IN PARTNERSHIP WITH CTᴇ LEARNING

This book was written with the support of https://www.ctelearning.com for all your career and technical education needs.

The eBook you've purchased will prepare you for the bootstrap section of their courseware. Allowing you to rapidly gain industry certifications.

Visit https://www.ctelearning.com/b5f/ for a list of courses supported by this eBook, as well as other training opportunities.

Enjoying working from home? Wish to continue remote working for the duration and after the pandemic? Try the CTᴇLearning remote professional freelancer course.

DEDICATION

To my love Diana, it is for you that I work hard daily.

To my father, who taught me knowledge is king.

To my mother, who put up with us both!

PREFACE

Welcome to the Bootstrap 5 Foundations book. This book is designed to teach you how to develop fast, responsive mobile-first websites.

When I first started learning to develop websites, I took the long way. I started with HTML5, learned CSS, and leapt to JavaScript. I attempted to work out all the media queries and responsive designs required to make a modern website work across multiple devices.

I took a very simplistic "I should know everything" approach to learning, which delayed my ability to produce an effective deployable website for a long time. While this makes me a great teacher, and a pedantic source of knowledge, it did not do what web developers are supposed to do—make websites!

Luckily for you, Bootstrap means you don't have to be an expert in CSS to make great-looking websites. You only need a very basic CSS knowledge and a good HTML5 knowledge.

Learning HTML5 is certainly not a step you should skip— the elements' names have real purpose with wide-ranging effects that go beyond how a website simply looks, and into SEO, accessibility and machine understanding of your site.

If you have a good solid understanding of HTML5, and a little CSS knowledge, you will be able to achieve a great-looking website with this book.

THE AUTHOR

Hello, I've been a technical education writer for nearly a decade, having produced many courses, videos, and more recently literature and podcasts.

I'm a growing social media influencer, with the majority of my followers on TikTok. Where I make unique informative and opinion driven content for the platform along with some humour.

https://www.tiktok.com/@ckenthusiast

I also write, host and run the podcast The RKE which you can find on Spotify.

https://open.spotify.com/show/4lfvnRht5hHrelGAddDQ9Z

Finally, I write technical industry standard courses which are taught worldwide in schools, colleges and universities. You can find these sold through my business partner's website.

www.ctelearning.com

And professional training courses which are sold through:

https://webprofessionalsglobal.org/

An industry certification company of professional web developers.

These projects, associations and business connects are the result of many years working for the industry and I'm excited to expand my product into the eBook domain.

WEB HOSTING

In addition to writing books, and producing educational content I run a web hosting and development service called Foreman Technology.

Foreman Technology is a web development, and web hosting company.

We offer a range of well-priced hosting services, and domain registration services. Along with design services.

In addition to standard web hosting packages, dedicated Wordpress, e-mail services, SSL certificates and other web support services are available.

Please visit www.foremantechnology.com and purchase your web hosting package today.

- Domains
- Linux/ Windows Hosting
- SSL
- E-Mail servers
- Web Design
- Wordpress hosting
- No-Coding website building

TABLE OF CONTENT

CONTENTS

In partnership with CTᵉ Learning 2

Dedication 2

Preface 3

The Author 4

Web Hosting 5

Table of Content 6

About the book 10

    Why be a front-end web developer? 11

        The money 11

        The fame 11

        The Power 11

    What do I need? 11

    Why Bootstrap 5? 12

        Requirements 13

        What is Bootstrap? 14

        Bootstrap versions 15

        Teaching bleeding edge technology 16

        What's new in Bootstrap 5? 17

Getting Started with Bootstrap 5 18

    Example 1 19

    Example 2 20

    Example 3 21

    Example 4 22

Bootstrap is a CSS class system 23

Typography 25

    Headings Typography 26

        Example 5 27

        Example 6 29

        Example 7 30

Heading classes 31
    Example 8 32

A note about SEO 34

Secondary heading text 35
    Example 9 36
    Example 10 37

Display Headings 38
    Example 11 39
    Example 12 41

Creating Lead Text 43
    Example 13 44
    Example 14 45

Text Alignment 47
    Example 15 48

Font Sizing 51
    Example 16 52
    Example 17 53

Text Styles and weight 54
    Example 18 56

Text Line-height 57
    Example 19 58

Text Transform 59
    Example 20 60

Underline strikethrough and removal of underline. 61
    Example 21 62

Lists 63
    Example 22 64

Bootstrap Colours 65
    Example 23 67

Borders 68
    Example 24 69
    Example 25 70

- Margins 71
    - Example 26 72
    - Example 27 73
- Padding 75
    - Example 28 76
    - Example 29 77
- Bootstrap Buttons 78
    - Example 30 78
    - Example 31 80
- Bootstrap Buttons with outlines 81
    - Example 32 82
    - Example 33 83
- End of section activity 84

Responsive Layout 85
- Bootstrap Containers 86
    - Example 34 87
- Bootstrap containers with breakpoints 88
    - Example 35 89
- Fluid Container 90
    - Example 36 91
- Bootstrap Grid System 92
    - Example 37 93
    - Example 38 94
    - Example 39 95
- Column breakpoints 96
    - Example 40 97
- Column Sizing 98
    - Example 41 99
- Column sizing and breakpoints 102
    - Example 42 104
- Images 106
    - Example 43 107

Cards 108

    Example 44 113

Gutters 115

    Example 45 116

    Example 46 118

    Example 47 121

Nav 124

    Example 48 128

Footer 131

    Example 49 133

End of section activity 136

The next step in your career 137

Index 138

ABOUT THE BOOK

This is not just any old eBook, it is a career building tool that will open doorways for you.

The knowledge in this book can be traded up for a professional association's international certification with The Web Professionals Association.

This book will prepare you for the world of responsive mobile first web design. Teaching the very latest (as of the date of publishing) version of Bootstrap 5, which you will learn about soon.

You can download the support files for this book from.

https://foremanlearning.com

WHY BE A FRONT-END WEB DEVELOPER?

The money, the fame, and the power! The understanding of all that is web, and the ability to understand how the world's largest interconnected network delivers information to its users worldwide.

THE MONEY

In an entry level position, the average UK salary starts at £28,000—and if you wish to work in the states (as I do) from the comfort of your own home, you could be earning anywhere from $58,000 to $76,929 annually. Freelancers can charge $67 an hour at the low end, and hundreds at the high end.

THE FAME

How do most people discover celebrities, entrepreneurs and influencers? The web! Knowing how to reach people through a great website, integrate your social media and control your own narrative is an important asset when creating an online presence. Companies are often based on the personality and character they present.

THE POWER

Too many managers, entrepreneurs and business owners depend on the internet to spread the word about their products and services but have almost zero knowledge of it. As you rise through the ranks of your company, or build a company of your own, you can approach tasks with a developer's mindset. You will be able to communicate on an equal footing with your development team as well as understand how they get things done and what they need to make your business succeed. Never underestimate a manager with a technical background. They make projects succeed.

WHAT DO I NEED?

While all examples are provided in this eBook you may wish to download the project files at:

https://www.ctelearning.com/b5f

Please visit this location to download.

You will need your favourite IDE. I use these cross platform free tools.

https://code.visualstudio.com/

http://brackets.io/

https://atom.io/

For Chromebooks you can use the online IDE:

http://www.cloudcodepro.com/

For iPhone and iPad:

https://koderapp.com/

For Android:

https://play.google.com/store/apps/details?id=com.aor.droidedit&hl=en_GB&gl=US

https://play.google.com/store/apps/details?id=xyz.iridiumion.enlightened&hl=en&gl=US

For Kindle Fire Tablets:

https://www.amazon.com/AWD-IDE-Code-Editor-WEB/dp/B00H5XSUKW

WHY BOOTSTRAP 5?

Bootstrap 5 is a mobile-first framework for building websites and applications. Bootstrap was conceived by Mark Otto and Jacob Thornton, who were working at Twitter in 2010. The project was released in 2011 as open source. Since then, Bootstrap has become a highly popular framework due to its ease of use and ability to deliver cross-platform compatibility between many browsers and devices.

Bootstrap has received over six hundred contributors to its codebase and has over 34,000 forks on GitHub.

Bootstrap is required learning if you are pursuing a career as a front-end web developer, as it allows easy collaboration between team members thanks to the universal layout tools, class names and common library functions.

Bootstrap 5 has moved away from jQuery, which it was previously heavily reliant on. Instead Bootstrap relies on JavaScript alone, making it easier to learn than ever before.

Whether you plan to make templates for a living, or become a full stack developer, understanding Bootstrap will go a long way in your career.

REQUIREMENTS

Bootstrap is a front-end mobile-first responsive framework because you won't have to create complicated classes of your own; you won't need advanced knowledge of CSS or JavaScript. However, it is recommended that you have a good understanding of HTML5 before you proceed.

This course will assume you are familiar with:

- HTML5
    - HTML Elements
    - HTML Attributes
    - Event handlers
- CSS3
    - Class selectors
    - Multiple class selectors .class1.class2 .class1 .class2, etc.
    - ID selectors #
    - Wildcard selectors *
    - Element selectors div, p, body, etc.
    - Multiple Element selectors div h1, body h1, etc.
    - Basic CSS3 rules, colour, background, etc.
- A basic awareness of JavaScript
    - What JavaScript is
    - What JavaScript is used for
    - How to load Scripts into a page

WHAT IS BOOTSTRAP?

Bootstrap is a free front-end development framework initially produced by a developer at Twitter and has since gone on to become one of the most popular mobile-first frameworks.

A framework is a tool that provides generic functionality between projects. It features a consistent API and naming structure that allow you to call upon and perform tasks rapidly, regardless of the project you are working on. Anyone trained in a framework can modify and manipulate existing projects with minimal training.

Bootstrap uses HTML5 as the means to create content, and Bootstrap adds many CSS classes that can be assigned to those elements. In addition to this, JavaScript code has been provided to deliver specific functionality.

- Accessibility
- Buttons
- Carousels
- Forms
- Images
- Modals
- Navigation
- Tables
- Typography

These are just a few of the features.

BOOTSTRAP VERSIONS

There are three major versions of Bootstrap in circulation: Bootstrap 3, 4 and 5. Versions 1 and 2 are no longer used in any meaningful way. So, we can ignore these. You can still find templates for 3, 4 and 5, however.

You should only use 3 if you really want to support old aging web browsers like Internet Explorer 8 and 9. Some institutions like the British NHS, which famously still uses Windows XP, do still use these browsers. If you are doing a job for a client with older browsers who isn't willing to update, usage of Bootstrap 3 is best.

Bootstrap 4.6 is the current version of Bootstrap. It supports Internet Explorer 10 and 11 but is being replaced with Bootstrap 5.0 soon. The need for Internet Explorer 10 and 11 is rapidly diminishing.

TEACHING BLEEDING EDGE TECHNOLOGY

Because it is important to prepare students for the very latest technology and to give this course and its knowledge the longest possible use, we will be teaching 5.0 Beta 2 of Bootstrap so that you are fully prepared to use it when entering the job market. Employers more often than not require the most up-to-date skills. What we are describing is a process called future proofing, which means learning a technology before or soon after it has been released to allow you to react faster to an ever-evolving market.

WHAT'S NEW IN BOOTSTRAP 5?

Bootstrap 5 is the latest version of the framework. Previous versions of Bootstrap have used jQuery, a JavaScript library that is designed to make JavaScript coding easier and faster. However, its main drawback is you can't simply use pre-existing Vanilla JavaScript knowledge. You must learn it.

jQuery came about in 2006 at a time when browsers did not cooperate very well with each other. jQuery allowed features to be transferable between different platforms. Since then, web standards and browser supported features have moved closer together, so it is easier than ever to use languages like CSS and JavaScript as they were intended.

Bootstrap 5 broke away from jQuery and stopped supporting Internet Explorer 10 and 11, which has been replaced with Microsoft Edge. It is designed with the latest version of web browsers.

Since the web has fully evolved past the need for jQuery, it has been removed from the latest version of Bootstrap.

GETTING STARTED WITH BOOTSTRAP 5

To make use of Bootstrap 5 you need the following:

- Knowledge of HTML5.
- Knowledge of HTML Attributes.
- Knowledge of classes.
- An HTML editor.
- A link to Bootstrap's CSS file.
- A link to the Bootstrap JavaScript file.
- The minimum HTML5 HTML file.

You will need to know HTML5 and how to assign class attributes. An understanding of HTML5 IDs is also useful. You will need to know how to use a HTML editor and create a basic HTML5 page.

Let's begin with the HTML5 page.

EXAMPLE 1

```
1.  <!doctype html>
2.  <html lang="en">
3.
4.      <head>
5.          <title>Minimal HTML5 page</title>
6.      </head>
7.
8.      <body>
9.          <h1>Minimal HTML5 page</h1>
10.         <p>This is the minimum code required to hit the HTML5 standards.</p>
11.     </body>
12.
13. </html>
```

This is the minimum code we need for a page. Now we are going to add Bootstrap to the mix.

The CSS link for Bootstrap is:

```
1.  <link href="https://cdn.jsdelivr.net/npm/bootstrap@5.0.0-beta3/dist/css/bootstrap.min.css" rel="stylesheet" crossorigin="anonymous">
```

Let's add this to our document.

EXAMPLE 2

```
1.  <!doctype html>
2.  <html lang="en">
3.
4.      <head>
5.          <title>Minimal Bootstrap 5 page</title>
6.          <link href="https://cdn.jsdelivr.net/npm/bootstrap@5.0.0-beta3/dist/css/bootstrap.min.css" rel="stylesheet" crossorigin="anonymous">
7.      </head>
8.
9.      <body>
10.         <h1>Minimal Bootstrap 5 page</h1>
11.         <p>This is the minimum code required to hit the HTML5 standards.</p>
12.     </body>
13.
14. </html>
```

Next, we add the JavaScript library, the link for this:

```
1.  <script src="https://cdn.jsdelivr.net/npm/bootstrap@5.0.0-beta3/dist/js/bootstrap.bundle.min.js" crossorigin="anonymous"></script>
```

We add that to the end of our template, before the last </body> element.

EXAMPLE 3

```
1.  <!doctype html>
2.  <html lang="en">
3.
4.      <head>
5.          <title>Minimal Bootstrap 5 page</title>
6.          <link href="https://cdn.jsdelivr.net/npm/bootstrap@5.0.0-beta3/dist/css/bootstrap.min.css" rel="stylesheet" crossorigin="anonymous">
7.      </head>
8.
9.      <body>
10.         <h1>Minimal Bootstrap 5 page</h1>
11.         <p>This is the minimum code required to hit the HTML5 standards.</p>
12.         <script src="https://cdn.jsdelivr.net/npm/bootstrap@5.0.0-beta3/dist/js/bootstrap.bundle.min.js" crossorigin="anonymous"></script>
13.     </body>
14.
15. </html>
```

This is the minimum we need for a Bootstrap template. However, it is good practice to set the viewport and charset of the document. By doing this, we ensure full compatibility.

```
1.  <meta charset="utf-8">
2.  <meta name="viewport" content="width=device-width, initial-scale=1">
```

We add this after the <title> element.

EXAMPLE 4

```html
1.  <!doctype html>
2.  <html lang="en">
3.  
4.  <head>
5.      <title>Minimal Bootstrap 5 page</title>
6.      <meta charset="utf-8">
7.      <meta name="viewport" content="width=device-width, initial-scale=1">
8.      <link href="https://cdn.jsdelivr.net/npm/bootstrap@5.0.0-beta3/dist/css/bootstrap.min.css" rel="stylesheet" crossorigin="anonymous">
9.  </head>
10. 
11. <body>
12.     <h1>Minimal Bootstrap 5 page</h1>
13.     <p>This is the minimum code required to hit the HTML5 standards.</p>
14.     <script src="https://cdn.jsdelivr.net/npm/bootstrap@5.0.0-beta3/dist/js/bootstrap.bundle.min.js" crossorigin="anonymous"></script>
15. </body>
16. 
17. </html>
18. 
```

Now that we have this template, we are ready to begin using Bootstrap.

BOOTSTRAP IS A CSS CLASS SYSTEM

Bootstrap works by taking standard HTML elements and assigning pre-written CSS classes to them. To use Bootstrap, you need to know the class names. The basic class names, in alphabetical order are:

- active
- alert
- align
- badge
- bg
- blockquote
- border
- btn
- card
- carousel
- clearfix
- close
- Col
- container
- custom
- d
- display
- drop
- embed
- fade
- fixed
- float
- font
- form
- h
- has
- initialism
- input
- invalid-feedback
- is
- justify-content
- lead
- list
- m
- mark
- modal
- nav
- next
- no
- offset
- order
- P
- page
- position
- progress
- rounded
- row
- shadow
- sr-only

- stretched
- success
- tab
- table
- tooltip
- visible
- w
- was-validated

You don't have to remember all of these right now—classes will be explored individually as we use them.

To use a class with an element you'll need to use the code `<div class="border">` and insert the class name between the double quotes. The border class adds a thin border around any element.

TYPOGRAPHY

Websites are mostly about the written word, embedded image/ video and layout. While some interactivity comes along for the ride that tends to push the art into app development rather than website development.

The typography section of this eBook will give you everything you need to make beautiful written content.

You will learn:

- Bootstrap Typography.
- Styling Techniques.
- Whitespace management.
- A little SEO optimization.
- Border control.
- Colours and their meanings.
- How to create and manage buttons and links.

HEADINGS TYPOGRAPHY

Bootstrap provides classes and styles for all standard HTML heading levels 1 through 6. These are assigned to standard element selectors within the Bootstrap framework. Bootstrap uses element selectors to style the <h1> to <h6> elements.

When using headings, you must maintain the correct structure, and you must only use a single h1 on a page. The h1 must mirror the content of the title element.

If you call your page Hotel Destination America, then your first and only <h1> element must announce the same name. This is because SEO (search engine optimization) checks to see if they match, which prevents web developers from misrepresenting the content of their web page.

In the early days of the web, it was possible for a developer selling tyres to see a trend on the web for a famous singer or actor then write a title like "You won't believe what happened to" and then put their tyre sales page up instead. It was a cheap and easy way to gain traffic to the site and get some sales.

To make your site accessible to as many users as possible, you need to ensure that heading structures are used in the correct way, which means you can use as many <h2> headings after the first <h1> but you may not jump to <h4> just because you like the style and look. The way headings look serve a purpose. The user needs to understand which heading belongs to which group.

EXAMPLE 5
Google Chrome renders headings on Windows 10 that look like this.

Heading Level 1

Heading Level 2

Heading Level 3

Heading Level 4

Heading Level 5

Heading Level 6

Using the following standard code:

```
1.  <!doctype html>
2.  <html lang="en">
3.
4.  <head>
5.      <title>Standard Heading's Chrome</title>
6.      <meta charset="utf-8">
7.      <meta name="viewport" content="width=device-width, initial-scale=1">
8.  </head>
9.
10. <body>
11.     <h1>Heading Level 1</h1>
12.     <h2>Heading Level 2</h2>
13.     <h3>Heading Level 3</h3>
14.     <h4>Heading Level 4</h4>
15.     <h5>Heading Level 5</h5>
16.     <h6>Heading Level 6</h6>
17. </body>
18.
19. </html>
```

The above example does not use Bootstrap in any way. You will see the browser's native rendering.

EXAMPLE 6

When we load Bootstrap, which you can see on the right-hand side, Bootstrap automatically styles the h elements, so you don't need to use the classes.

Pure HTML

Heading Level 1
Heading Level 2
Heading Level 3
Heading Level 4
Heading Level 5
Heading Level 6

Bootstrap 5 styled

Heading Level 1
Heading Level 2
Heading Level 3
Heading Level 4
Heading Level 5
Heading Level 6

As you can see, the Bootstrap headings have less spacing between them, and a different font. Bootstrap uses a font stack that looks similar on every major device including Windows, MacOS, iOS, Android, and Linux.

```
1.  <!doctype html>
2.  <html lang="en">
3.
4.  <head>
5.      <title>Minimal Bootstrap 5 page</title>
6.      <meta charset="utf-8">
7.      <meta name="viewport" content="width=device-width, initial-scale=1">
8.      <link href="https://cdn.jsdelivr.net/npm/bootstrap@5.0.0-beta3/dist/css/bootstrap.min.css" rel="stylesheet" crossorigin="anonymous">
9.  </head>
10.
11. <body>
12.     <h1>Heading Level 1</h1>
13.     <h2>Heading Level 2</h2>
14.     <h3>Heading Level 3</h3>
15.     <h4>Heading Level 4</h4>
16.     <h5>Heading Level 5</h5>
17.     <h6>Heading Level 6</h6>
18.     <script src="https://cdn.jsdelivr.net/npm/bootstrap@5.0.0-beta3/dist/js/bootstrap.bundle.min.js" crossorigin="anonymous"></script>
19. </body>
20.
21. </html>
```

EXAMPLE 7

This is an example of headings being properly formatted. We start with a <h1> element that announces the name of the page, then we have a series of <h> series elements that are in order. We never jump from 2 to 4 or from 1 to 3. We always go in a leading structure.

```html
1.  <!doctype html>
2.  <html lang="en">
3.  
4.  <head>
5.      <title>Heading structure</title>
6.      <meta charset="utf-8">
7.      <meta name="viewport" content="width=device-width, initial-scale=1">
8.      <link href="https://cdn.jsdelivr.net/npm/bootstrap@5.0.0-beta3/dist/css/bootstrap.min.css" rel="stylesheet" >
9.  </head>
10. 
11. <body>
12.     <h1>Heading Structure</h1>
13.     <h2>Topic 1</h2>
14.     <h3>Topic 1.1</h3>
15.     <h4>Topic 1.1.1</h4>
16.     <h4>Topic 1.1.2</h4>
17.     <h5>Topic 1.1.2.1</h5>
18.     <h6>Topic 1.1.2.1.1</h6>
19.     <h3>Topic 1.2</h3>
20.     <h4>Topic 1.2.1</h4>
21.     <h2>Topic 2</h2>
22.     <h3>Topic 2.1</h3>
23.     <h3>Topic 2.2</h3>
24.     <h2>Topic 3</h2>
25.     <h3>Topic 3.1</h3>
26.     <script src="https://cdn.jsdelivr.net/npm/bootstrap@5.0.0-beta3/dist/js/bootstrap.bundle.min.js"></script>
27. </body>
28. 
29. </html>
```

HEADING CLASSES

In addition to the default <h1> to <h6> elements being styled, we have access to the same styles with the same names using class selectors rather than element selectors. This allows the developer to fake headings if they need to. In some applications this can be required, especially when generating custom elements.

However, it is bad practice to do this normally, as the HTML5 standard carries meaning when you use the H1 to H6 element structure. Disabled users, bots, and automated systems often need the right element to be used in the right situation.

While it is possible to use classes on non-heading elements, there should be no need to do so in a properly ordered and robust HTML5 document.

EXAMPLE 8

Heading Level 1

Heading Level 1 (fake)

Heading Level 2

Heading Level 2 (fake)

Heading Level 3

Heading Level 3 (fake)

Heading Level 4

Heading Level 4 (fake)

Heading Level 5

Heading Level 5 (fake)

Heading Level 6

Heading Level 6 (fake)

We created a document that uses both the H elements, and a paragraph with the style applied. As you can see, there is no visual difference between the two. To indicate the difference between them, we've placed the fake in brackets afterward.

The class is simply applied using the standard class attribute.

```html
1.  <!doctype html>
2.  <html lang="en">
3.  
4.  <head>
5.      <title>Minimal Bootstrap 5 page</title>
6.      <meta charset="utf-8">
7.      <meta name="viewport" content="width=device-width, initial-scale=1">
8.      <link href="https://cdn.jsdelivr.net/npm/bootstrap@5.0.0-beta3/dist/css/bootstrap.min.css" rel="stylesheet" crossorigin="anonymous">
9.  </head>
10. 
11. <body>
12.     <h1>Heading Level 1</h1>
13.     <p class="h1">Heading Level 1 (fake)</p>
14.     <h2>Heading Level 2</h2>
15.     <p class="h2">Heading Level 2 (fake)</p>
16.     <h3>Heading Level 3</h3>
17.     <p class="h3">Heading Level 3 (fake)</p>
18.     <h4>Heading Level 4</h4>
19.     <p class="h4">Heading Level 4 (fake)</p>
20.     <h5>Heading Level 5</h5>
21.     <p class="h5">Heading Level 5 (fake)</p>
22.     <h6>Heading Level 6</h6>
23.     <p class="h6">Heading Level 6 (fake)</p>
24.     <script src="https://cdn.jsdelivr.net/npm/bootstrap@5.0.0-beta3/dist/js/bootstrap.bundle.min.js" crossorigin="anonymous"></script>
25. </body>
26. 
27. </html>
28. 
```

It is worth noting that the code used above should not be used. While they are visually similar, creating a `<p class="h1">` would not carry the same meaning as using a true `<h1>` element.

A NOTE ABOUT SEO

SEO stands for Search Engine Optimization, and good SEO is the difference between placing your site at the top of a search engine and being buried hundreds of results in. If you do not appear on the top or at least on the first page of a search result then you will receive less web traffic, no matter how brilliant your site is.

SEO relies on trust. It is a common trick for less than honest developers to write a website claiming to be one thing, and then provide different content.

Say for example, a popular show is trending like *The Mandalorian*. You could easily write a website with the title "Top 10 Mandalorian scenes that will amaze you!" If a search engine finds it and says, "That's popular, let's push this page up the search rankings," you can quickly gain a lot of traffic.

That happened a lot in the old days of the internet.

Today however, some basic checks on trust are performed. One of these is that the website title must match the first <h1> found in the document.

If your website title is "Top 10 Mandalorian scenes that will amaze you!" and your <h1> says "Get out of debt with these 10 credit cards," then the search engine will not trust the site. To help ensure trust, the <h1> must repeat what the website title states. If they don't match, your site is treated as suspicious and pushed down the search rankings.

In addition to this, if you used a `<p class="h1">` or a `<span class="h1">` or anything that isn't a <h1> element, then the bot looking at your site for SEO will not find it. Not having a H1 match your title is as bad as having mismatching titles and h1 elements.

Ensure that you use the <h1> element just once on your website and ensure that it has the same text as your title element.

SECONDARY HEADING TEXT

Sometimes you will want to create secondary text in your headings to provide extra information. To do this we have the .text-muted class. It is best placed in <small> elements which will reduce the size of the font in addition to changing the colour of the text.

```html
<h2>Top Tech Tips <small class="text-muted">for an amazing tech career</small></h2>
```

EXAMPLE 9

We use small because it does not change the meaning of the text in any meaningful way, nothing is emphasised, and nothing is marked as important. Splitting the styling can make the heading look more striking, and separate information that the user needs to know as part of the title. It is an attention grabber, and engages the reader's interest by visually separating the information.

This is best used on secondary and lower headings <h2> to <h6> so we don't risk affecting the SEO of the <h1> element, which should reflect the <title> element's textual content.

When used, the <h2> element looks like this:

Secondary headings

Top Tech Tips for an amazing tech career

Getting an amazing tech career will lead to much happiness!

```
1.  <!doctype html>
2.  <html lang="en">
3.
4.  <head>
5.      <title>Secondary headings</title>
6.      <meta charset="utf-8">
7.      <meta name="viewport" content="width=device-width, initial-scale=1">
8.      <link href="https://cdn.jsdelivr.net/npm/bootstrap@5.0.0-beta3/dist/css/bootstrap.min.css" rel="stylesheet" crossorigin="anonymous">
9.  </head>
10.
11. <body>
12.     <h1>Secondary headings</h1>
13.     <h2>Top Tech Tips <small class="text-muted">for an amazing tech career</small></h2>
14.     <p>Getting an amazing tech career will lead to much happiness!</p>
15.     <script src="https://cdn.jsdelivr.net/npm/bootstrap@5.0.0-beta3/dist/js/bootstrap.bundle.min.js" crossorigin="anonymous"></script>
16. </body>
17.
18. </html>
19.
```

EXAMPLE 10

Another example of separated but related information would be the pricing of a hotel room. In the example demonstrated below we can see that the price of the room is made distinct from the rest of the statement.

Hotel Rooms

Bay view room £500 + vat

Our amazing bay view room, gives views of the ships coming in and our of the harbour all year long.

```
1.  <!doctype html>
2.  <html lang="en">
3.
4.  <head>
5.      <title>Hotel Rooms</title>
6.      <meta charset="utf-8">
7.      <meta name="viewport" content="width=device-width, initial-scale=1">
8.      <link href="https://cdn.jsdelivr.net/npm/bootstrap@5.0.0-beta3/dist/css/bootstrap.min.css" rel="stylesheet" crossorigin="anonymous">
9.  </head>
10.
11. <body>
12.     <h1>Hotel Rooms</h1>
13.     <h2>Bay view room <small class="text-muted">£500 + vat</small></h2>
14.     <p>Our amazing bay view room, gives views of the ships coming in and our of the harbour all year long.</p>
15.     <script src="https://cdn.jsdelivr.net/npm/bootstrap@5.0.0-beta3/dist/js/bootstrap.bundle.min.js" crossorigin="anonymous"></script>
16. </body>
17.
18. </html>
```

DISPLAY HEADINGS

Display headings are a means of grabbing the user's attention with a big display. While the standard <h1> to <h6> levels should be maintained when organising a document, if you are providing a heading that needs a heavier presentation on the page then the .display-1 to .display-6 classes aid with this.

If you are promoting a message, a call to action, or other major feature on your site, display headings are very useful.

However, display headings do not change the nature of the element or the perceived importance of the heading level. Remember that heading levels have a strict hierarchy, you should never jump heading levels, and should always keep them organised. A single <h1> per page, matching the <title> followed by your headings and subheadings being present in levels 2 through to 6.

In addition to this, you should also ensure that people visually understand what level heading you are using. Don't make a level heading 6 match the style of a display-1, because you are not relaying the importance level of that heading.

A properly structured document improves SEO, readability and machine understanding of your page.

EXAMPLE 11

The following is an example of headings default next to display headings. You will see a dramatic difference between the two.

Heading 1

Display Heading 1

Heading 2

Display Heading 2

Heading 3

Display Heading 3

Heading 4

Display Heading 4

Heading 5

Display Heading 5

Heading 6

Display Heading 6

Display headings follow the same sizing scale as normal headings. The size denotes their level of importance, and it is essential that readers are able to identify the importance of a section. It improves readability and creates a robust document.

I would also recommend maintaining a single style. If your page is filled with display headings and normal headings, then their importance is not maintained. Their structure becomes visually messy.

```html
1.  <!doctype html>
2.  <html lang="en">
3.
4.  <head>
5.      <title>Display Headings</title>
6.      <meta charset="utf-8">
7.      <meta name="viewport" content="width=device-width, initial-scale=1">
8.      <link href="https://cdn.jsdelivr.net/npm/bootstrap@5.0.0-beta3/dist/css/bootstrap.min.css" rel="stylesheet" crossorigin="anonymous">
9.  </head>
10.
11. <body>
12.     <h1>Heading 1</h1>
13.     <h1 class="display-1">Display Heading 1</h1>
14.     <h2>Heading 2</h2>
15.     <h2 class="display-2">Display Heading 2</h2>
16.     <h3>Heading 3</h3>
17.     <h3 class="display-3">Display Heading 3</h3>
18.     <h4>Heading 4</h4>
19.     <h4 class="display-4">Display Heading 4</h4>
20.     <h5>Heading 5</h5>
21.     <h5 class="display-5">Display Heading 5</h5>
22.     <h6>Heading 6</h6>
23.     <h6 class="display-6">Display Heading 6</h6>
24. </body>
25.
26. </html>
```

EXAMPLE 12

If you do decide to mix them, try to keep the layout consistent. For example, below I've only used the display-1 and display-2 classes with heading level 1 and heading level 2. After that, heading level 3 was allowed to continue as standard.

Hotel Rooms

View our amazing range of hotel rooms!

West wing

Bay view room £500 + vat

Our amazing bay view room, gives views of the ships coming in and our of the harbour all year long.

Magpie view room £350 + vat

Our smaller magpie room, gives views of the migrating magpies six months of the year.

East wing

Mountain view room £475 + vat

Our mountain view room, allows you to spot wild life with the included telescope.

Magpie view room £300 + vat

Our medium magpie room, gives views of the migrating magpies six months of the year.

This was done because there is a clear hierarchy with the headings, plus the two promotional texts, what the page is, and which side of the building the rooms are on are clearly presented. The <h3> elements and secondary texts are then maintained as normal.

If a <h4> was to be used it should not use a display-4 after no display-3 was used, because the heading structure will visually lose its meaning.

```
1.  <!doctype html>
2.  <html lang="en">
3.
4.  <head>
5.      <title>Hotel Rooms</title>
6.      <meta charset="utf-8">
7.      <meta name="viewport" content="width=device-width, initial-scale=1">
8.      <link href="https://cdn.jsdelivr.net/npm/bootstrap@5.0.0-beta3/dist/css/bootstrap.min.css"
```

```html
       rel="stylesheet" crossorigin="anonymous">
 9.  </head>
10.
11.  <body>
12.      <h1 class="display-1">Hotel Rooms</h1>
13.      <p>View our amazing range of hotel rooms!</p>
14.
15.      <h2 class="display-2">West wing</h2>
16.      <h3>Bay view room <small class="text-muted">£500 + vat</small></h3>
17.      <p>Our amazing bay view room, gives views of the ships coming in and our of the harbour all year long.</p>
18.      <h3>Magpie view room <small class="text-muted">£350 + vat</small></h3>
19.      <p>Our smaller magpie room, gives views of the migrating magpies six months of the year.</p>
20.      <h2 class="display-2">East wing</h2>
21.      <h3>Mountain view room <small class="text-muted">£475 + vat</small></h3>
22.      <p>Our mountain view room, allows you to spot wild life with the included telescope.</p>
23.      <h3>Magpie view room <small class="text-muted">£300 + vat</small></h3>
24.      <p>Our medium magpie room, gives views of the migrating magpies six months of the year.</p>
25.      <script src="https://cdn.jsdelivr.net/npm/bootstrap@5.0.0-beta3/dist/js/bootstrap.bundle.min.js" crossorigin="anonymous"></script>
26.  </body>
27.
28.  </html>
```

CREATING LEAD TEXT

A lead paragraph is the opening paragraph of an article, essay, book chapter, blog, or anything else written. It provides a lighter gray visually distinctive text that grabs the reader's attention. It can be used to tease information or introduce or summarise text.

We use the lead class to assign the lead text to a paragraph.

It should only be used once per piece of writing, unless that writing is divided by headings—for example, multiple chapters in an eBook.

EXAMPLE 13

We have multiple paragraphs with leading texts, allowing readers to drift between interesting pieces of information. Room pricing, room names, locations in buildings and lead paragraphs further capture the attention of readers.

Hotel Rooms

View our amazing range of hotel rooms!

West wing

Bay view room £500 + vat

Our amazing bay view room, gives views of the ships coming in and out of the harbour all year long.

Our harbour is one of the busiest in the world. View the worlds fleet come and go about their business.

Magpie view room £350 + vat

Magpies have bold intelligence and personality, they are known for having chatters whistles thrills and warbles. Watch these amazing birds from the comfort of your room.

Our smaller magpie room, gives views of the migrating magpies six months of the year.

East wing

Mountain view room £475 + vat

View our stunning mountain side and the famous goats that graze upon them!

Our mountain view room, allows you to spot wild life with the included telescope.

Magpie view room £300 + vat

Our medium magpie room, gives views of the migrating magpies six months of the year.

Magpies have bold intelligence and personality, they are known for having chatters whistles thrills and warbles. Watch these amazing birds from the comfort of your room.

The lead text is used directly after the heading level announcing the topic. In this case a heading level <h3> appeared without a display class. It was then followed by the lead paragraph.

```
1.  <!doctype html>
2.  <html lang="en">
3.
4.  <head>
5.      <title>Hotel Rooms</title>
6.      <meta charset="utf-8">
7.      <meta name="viewport" content="width=device-width, initial-scale=1">
8.      <link href="https://cdn.jsdelivr.net/npm/bootstrap@5.0.0-beta3/dist/css/bootstrap.min.css" rel="stylesheet" crossorigin="anonymous">
9.  </head>
10.
11. <body>
12.     <h1 class="display-1">Hotel Rooms</h1>
13.     <p>View our amazing range of hotel rooms!</p>
14.     <h2 class="display-2">West wing</h2>
15.     <h3>Bay view room <small class="text-muted">£500 + vat</small></h3>
16.     <p class="lead">Our amazing bay view room, gives views of the ships coming in and our of the harbour all year long.</p>
17.     <p>Our harbour is one of the busiest in the world. View the worlds fleet come and go about their business.</p>
18.     <h3>Magpie view room <small class="text-muted">£350 + vat</small></h3>
19.     <p class="lead">Magpies have bold intelligence and personality, they are known for having chatters whistles thrills and warbles. Watch these amazing birds from the comfort of your room.</p>
20.     <p>Our smaller magpie room, gives views of the migrating magpies six months of the year.</p>
21.     <h2 class="display-2">East wing</h2>
22.     <h3>Mountain view room <small class="text-muted">£475 + vat</small></h3>
23.     <p class="lead">View our stunning mountain side and the famous goats that graze upon them!</p>
```

```
24.     <p>Our mountain view room, allows you to spot wild life with the included telescope.</p>
25.     <h3>Magpie view room <small class="text-muted">£300 + vat</small></h3>
26.     <p class="lead">Our medium magpie room, gives views of the migrating magpies six months of the year.</p>
27.     <p>Magpies have bold intelligence and personality, they are known for having chatters whistles thrills and warbles. Watch these amazing birds from the comfort of your room.</p>
28.     <script src="https://cdn.jsdelivr.net/npm/bootstrap@5.0.0-beta3/dist/js/bootstrap.bundle.min.js" crossorigin="anonymous"></script>
29. </body>
30.
31. </html>
```

EXAMPLE 14

Another example of leading text would be the famous novel *The War of the Worlds*, which is out of copyright and thus free to use.

This book has one of the most famously quoted opening lines, which we can highlight in the use of the lead class.

War of the worlds

No one would have believed in the last years of the nineteenth century that this world was being watched keenly and closely by intelligences greater than man's and yet as mortal as his own.

That as men busied themselves about their various concerns they were scrutinised and studied, perhaps almost as narrowly as a man with a microscope might scrutinise the transient creatures that swarm and multiply in a drop of water. With infinite complacency men went to and fro over this globe about their little affairs, serene in their assurance of their empire over matter. It is possible that the infusoria under the microscope do the same. No one gave a thought to the older worlds of space as sources of human danger, or thought of them only to dismiss the idea of life upon them as impossible or improbable. It is curious to recall some of the mental habits of those departed days. At most terrestrial men fancied there might be other men upon Mars, perhaps inferior to themselves and ready to welcome a missionary enterprise. Yet across the gulf of space, minds that are to our minds as ours are to those of the beasts that perish, intellects vast and cool and unsympathetic, regarded this earth with envious eyes, and slowly and surely drew their plans against us. And early in the twentieth century came the great disillusionment.

The planet Mars, I scarcely need remind the reader, revolves about the sun at a mean distance of 140,000,000 miles, and the light and heat it receives from the sun is barely half of that received by this world. It must be, if the nebular hypothesis has any truth, older than our world; and long before this earth ceased to be molten, life upon its surface must have begun its course. The fact that it is scarcely one seventh of the volume of the earth must have accelerated its cooling to the temperature at which life could begin. It has air and water and all that is necessary for the support of animated existence.

Leading this chapter with that famously quoted opening line helps to draw the user in.

```
1.  <!doctype html>
2.  <html lang="en">
3.
4.  <head>
5.      <title>War of the Worlds</title>
6.      <meta charset="utf-8">
7.      <meta name="viewport" content="width=device-width, initial-scale=1">
8.      <link href="https://cdn.jsdelivr.net/npm/bootstrap@5.0.0-beta3/dist/css/bootstrap.min.css" rel="stylesheet" crossorigin="anonymous">
9.  </head>
10.
11. <body>
12.     <h1 class="display-1">War of the worlds</h1>
13.     <p class="lead">No one would have believed in the last years of the nineteenth century that this world was being watched keenly and closely by intelligences greater than man's and yet as mortal as his own.</p>
14.     <p>That as men busied themselves about their various concerns they were scrutinised and studied, perhaps almost as narrowly as a man with a microscope might scrutinise the transient creatures that swarm and multiply in a drop of water. With infinite complacency men went to and fro over this globe about their little affairs, serene in their assurance of their empire over matter. It is possible that the infusoria under the microscope do the same. No one gave a thought to the older worlds of space as sources of human danger, or thought of them only to dismiss the idea of life upon them as impossible or improbable. It is curious to recall some of the mental habits of those departed days. At most terrestrial men fancied there might be other men upon Mars, perhaps inferior to themselves and ready to welcome a missionary enterprise. Yet across the gulf of space, minds that are to our minds as ours are to those of the beasts that perish, intellects vast and cool and unsympathetic, regarded this earth with envious eyes, and slowly and surely drew their plans against us. And early in the twentieth century came the great disillusionment.</p>
15.     <p>The planet Mars, I scarcely need remind the reader, revolves about the sun at a mean distance of
```

140,000,000 miles, and the light and heat it receives from the sun is barely half of that received by this world. It must be, if the nebular hypothesis has any truth, older than our world; and long before this earth ceased to be molten, life upon its surface must have begun its course. The fact that it is scarcely one seventh of the volume of the earth must have accelerated its cooling to the temperature at which life could begin. It has air and water and all that is necessary for the support of animated existence.</p>
16. </body>
17. </html>

TEXT ALIGNMENT

To align text to left, centre or right gives you the option of visually styling or aligning your text for formatting and layout reasons. When using a word processor, we have the Align Left, Center and Right Align options. Bootstrap refers to them a little differently.

- Start Align
- End Align
- Center Align

They are assigned using the classes text-start, text-end and text-center.

In most word processors there is also the option to fully justify the text. The problem with the full justify method is that it creates an uneven spacing between words. There are some users who find this difficult to read, so the Bootstrap team decided to leave the option out.

EXAMPLE 15

In this example we are aligning text using the text-center, text-start and text-end classes. This paragraph will align to the center.

```
1.      <p class="text-center">Ut eget erat ac felis lacinia porta a id neque. Mauris sagittis efficitur orci
non interdum. Nulla id augue mauris. Mauris in semper mi, tincidunt suscipit urna. Integer metus sapien,
aliquet quis sem vel, rutrum aliquam orci. Duis ornare finibus diam a fermentum. Aenean interdum purus vel
aliquam ullamcorper. Quisque maximus semper libero et convallis. Morbi tristique lobortis magna, vel varius
quam gravida eu. Nunc pharetra leo nisl, eu convallis sapien viverra quis. Praesent semper, nunc in vehicula
imperdiet, diam erat ullamcorper ipsum, facilisis faucibus ligula ipsum ut lorem. Fusce sagittis maximus orci
in varius. Integer laoreet viverra tortor. Nulla iaculis ipsum in nulla pretium accumsan. Suspendisse quis
magna auctor, sodales elit at, rutrum sem. Nullam sit amet orci tincidunt, ullamcorper mi eget, bibendum
massa.</p>
```

This paragraph will be aligned to the left like normal, so unless you have previously used a text alignment this will not change anything.

```
1. <p class="text-start">Lorem ipsum dolor sit amet, consectetur adipiscing elit. Suspendisse dapibus
lobortis venenatis. Sed risus tortor, aliquet et odio et, auctor elementum massa. Vivamus tristique libero
sit amet placerat posuere. Pellentesque a est scelerisque, aliquam est ut, rhoncus odio. Curabitur sed
maximus erat. Nam vestibulum non tortor nec tristique. Nam fringilla rhoncus accumsan. Vestibulum ante ipsum
primis in faucibus orci luctus et ultrices posuere cubilia curae; Aliquam congue, leo in fermentum venenatis,
lorem nibh tincidunt ipsum, ut euismod turpis turpis varius odio. Nulla ullamcorper quis metus non bibendum.
In at turpis nec tortor dictum pharetra quis id ante. Cras ut nisl sagittis, blandit est eu, tincidunt
risus.</p>
```

Then we have the align to the right, which is text-end.

```
1. <p class="text-end">Integer quis dignissim leo. Nunc tincidunt turpis leo, id hendrerit augue lacinia
quis. Maecenas egestas odio turpis, nec rhoncus dolor consectetur eu. Curabitur ut rutrum tellus. In nisi
diam, vestibulum eget est ut, ultricies euismod ante. Aenean sit amet odio pulvinar, ornare ante id, sagittis
nisi. Phasellus luctus nisi eu nibh ornare bibendum. Ut porttitor rutrum tortor non pharetra. Nam eget ligula
non urna cursus volutpat. Vivamus in risus lacinia, fermentum mi molestie, dictum sem. Suspendisse
scelerisque maximus nisl, maximus ullamcorper ante vulputate vel. Aenean id purus metus. Maecenas sed mauris
sagittis, pulvinar dolor interdum, laoreet ante. Praesent fermentum commodo elit, vel ullamcorper tortor
sodales placerat. Curabitur ante mauris, elementum quis mattis eget, suscipit et nisi. Integer vitae dolor
pellentesque, euismod lacus at, molestie ex.</p>
```

When rendered, the aligned text looks like this.

Text Alignment

Start Aligned

Lorem ipsum dolor sit amet, consectetur adipiscing elit. Suspendisse dapibus lobortis venenatis. Sed risus tortor, aliquet et odio et, auctor elementum massa. Vivamus tristique libero sit amet placerat posuere. Pellentesque a est scelerisque, aliquam est ut, rhoncus odio. Curabitur sed maximus erat. Nam vestibulum non tortor nec tristique. Nam fringilla rhoncus accumsan. Vestibulum ante ipsum primis in faucibus orci luctus et ultrices posuere cubilia curae; Aliquam congue, leo in fermentum venenatis, lorem nibh tincidunt ipsum, ut euismod turpis turpis varius odio. Nulla ullamcorper quis metus non bibendum. In at turpis nec tortor dictum pharetra quis id ante. Cras ut nisl sagittis, blandit est eu, tincidunt risus.

Center Aligned

Ut eget erat ac felis lacinia porta a id neque. Mauris sagittis efficitur orci non interdum. Nulla id augue mauris. Mauris in semper mi, tincidunt suscipit urna. Integer metus sapien, aliquet quis sem vel, rutrum aliquam orci. Duis ornare finibus diam a fermentum. Aenean interdum purus vel aliquam ullamcorper. Quisque maximus semper libero et convallis. Morbi tristique lobortis magna, vel varius quam gravida eu. Nunc pharetra leo nisl, eu convallis sapien viverra quis. Praesent semper, nunc in vehicula imperdiet, diam erat ullamcorper ipsum, facilisis faucibus ligula ipsum ut lorem. Fusce sagittis maximus orci in varius. Integer laoreet viverra tortor. Nulla iaculis ipsum in nulla pretium accumsan. Suspendisse quis magna auctor, sodales elit at, rutrum sem. Nullam sit amet orci tincidunt, ullamcorper mi eget, bibendum massa.

End Aligned

Integer quis dignissim leo. Nunc tincidunt turpis leo, id hendrerit augue lacinia quis. Maecenas egestas odio turpis, nec rhoncus dolor consectetur eu. Curabitur ut rutrum tellus. In nisi diam, vestibulum eget est ut, ultricies euismod ante. Aenean sit amet odio pulvinar, ornare ante id, sagittis nisi. Phasellus luctus nisi eu nibh ornare bibendum. Ut porttitor rutrum tortor non pharetra. Nam eget ligula non urna cursus volutpat. Vivamus in risus lacinia, fermentum mi molestie, dictum sem. Suspendisse scelerisque maximus nisl, maximus ullamcorper ante vulputate vel. Aenean id purus metus. Maecenas sed mauris sagittis, pulvinar dolor interdum, laoreet ante. Praesent fermentum commodo elit, vel ullamcorper tortor sodales placerat. Curabitur ante mauris, elementum quis mattis eget, suscipit et nisi. Integer vitae dolor pellentesque, euismod lacus at, molestie ex.

When we combine it, we simply add it as a normal paragraph, as you can see in the example below.

```
1.  <!doctype html>
2.  <html lang="en">
3.
4.  <head>
5.      <title>Text Alignment</title>
6.      <meta charset="utf-8">
7.      <meta name="viewport" content="width=device-width, initial-scale=1">
8.      <link href="https://cdn.jsdelivr.net/npm/bootstrap@5.0.0-beta3/dist/css/bootstrap.min.css" rel="stylesheet">
9.  </head>
10.
11. <body class="p-2">
12.     <h1 class="display-1">Text Alignment</h1>
13.     <h2>Start Aligned</h2>
14.     <p class="text-start">Lorem ipsum dolor sit amet, consectetur adipiscing elit. Suspendisse dapibus lobortis venenatis. Sed risus tortor, aliquet et odio et, auctor elementum massa. Vivamus tristique libero sit amet placerat posuere. Pellentesque a est scelerisque, aliquam est ut, rhoncus odio. Curabitur sed maximus erat. Nam vestibulum non tortor nec tristique. Nam fringilla rhoncus accumsan. Vestibulum ante ipsum primis in faucibus orci luctus et ultrices posuere cubilia curae; Aliquam congue, leo in fermentum venenatis, lorem nibh tincidunt ipsum, ut euismod turpis turpis varius odio. Nulla ullamcorper quis metus non bibendum. In at turpis nec tortor dictum pharetra quis id ante. Cras ut nisl sagittis, blandit est eu, tincidunt risus.</p>
15.     <h2>Center Aligned</h2>
16.     <p class="text-center">Ut eget erat ac felis lacinia porta a id neque. Mauris sagittis efficitur orci non interdum. Nulla id augue mauris. Mauris in semper mi, tincidunt suscipit urna. Integer metus sapien, aliquet quis sem vel, rutrum aliquam orci. Duis ornare finibus diam a fermentum. Aenean interdum purus vel aliquam ullamcorper. Quisque maximus semper libero et convallis. Morbi tristique lobortis magna, vel varius
```

```
     quam gravida eu. Nunc pharetra leo nisl, eu convallis sapien viverra quis. Praesent semper, nunc in vehicula
     imperdiet, diam erat ullamcorper ipsum, facilisis faucibus ligula ipsum ut lorem. Fusce sagittis maximus orci
     in varius. Integer laoreet viverra tortor. Nulla iaculis ipsum in nulla pretium accumsan. Suspendisse quis
     magna auctor, sodales elit at, rutrum sem. Nullam sit amet orci tincidunt, ullamcorper mi eget, bibendum
     massa.</p>
17.      <h2>End Aligned</h2>
18.      <p class="text-end">Integer quis dignissim leo. Nunc tincidunt turpis leo, id hendrerit augue lacinia
     quis. Maecenas egestas odio turpis, nec rhoncus dolor consectetur eu. Curabitur ut rutrum tellus. In nisi
     diam, vestibulum eget est ut, ultricies euismod ante. Aenean sit amet odio pulvinar, ornare ante id, sagittis
     nisi. Phasellus luctus nisi eu nibh ornare bibendum. Ut porttitor rutrum tortor non pharetra. Nam eget ligula
     non urna cursus volutpat. Vivamus in risus lacinia, fermentum mi molestie, dictum sem. Suspendisse
     scelerisque maximus nisl, maximus ullamcorper ante vulputate vel. Aenean id purus metus. Maecenas sed mauris
     sagittis, pulvinar dolor interdum, laoreet ante. Praesent fermentum commodo elit, vel ullamcorper tortor
     sodales placerat. Curabitur ante mauris, elementum quis mattis eget, suscipit et nisi. Integer vitae dolor
     pellentesque, euismod lacus at, molestie ex.</p>
19.      <script src="https://cdn.jsdelivr.net/npm/bootstrap@5.0.0-
     beta3/dist/js/bootstrap.bundle.min.js"></script>
20.  </body>
21. </html>
```

FONT SIZING

We can change font sizes inside paragraphs, spans, strong, em, and other text elements that convey a special meaning, or simply display text. They can also be used to add a more dramatic appearance to a piece of text.

If you wish to make a stronger point, you can combine it with the strong element to embolden and make text stand out. This is good for warnings and important information.

As with heading levels 1 to 6, we have six levels of text.

We access them using the fs-1, fs-2, fs-3, fs-4, fs-5 and fs-6 classes.

The fs-6 class is the base font size—as you decrease the value, the text becomes larger.

EXAMPLE 16

Here we have an example of the sizes of text you have available.

```
1.      <h1 class="display-1">Font Sizing</h1>
2.      <p class="fs-1">Font Size 1</p>
3.      <p class="fs-2">Font Size 2</p>
4.      <p class="fs-3">Font Size 3</p>
5.      <p class="fs-4">Font Size 4</p>
6.      <p class="fs-5">Font Size 5</p>
7.      <p class="fs-6">Font Size 6</p>
```

When we render the page, we have text that looks like this:

Font Sizing

Font Size 1

Font Size 2

Font Size 3

Font Size 4

Font Size 5

Font Size 6

The entire source code looks like this.

```
1.  <!doctype html>
2.  <html lang="en">
3.
4.  <head>
5.      <title>Font Sizing</title>
6.      <meta charset="utf-8">
7.      <meta name="viewport" content="width=device-width, initial-scale=1">
8.      <link href="https://cdn.jsdelivr.net/npm/bootstrap@5.0.0-beta3/dist/css/bootstrap.min.css" rel="stylesheet" crossorigin="anonymous">
9.  </head>
10.
11. <body class="p-2">
12.     <h1 class="display-1">Font Sizing</h1>
13.     <p class="fs-1">Font Size 1</p>
14.     <p class="fs-2">Font Size 2</p>
15.     <p class="fs-3">Font Size 3</p>
16.     <p class="fs-4">Font Size 4</p>
17.     <p class="fs-5">Font Size 5</p>
18.     <p class="fs-6">Font Size 6</p>
19.     <script src="https://cdn.jsdelivr.net/npm/bootstrap@5.0.0-beta3/dist/js/bootstrap.bundle.min.js" crossorigin="anonymous"></script>
20. </body>
21. </html>
22.
```

EXAMPLE 17

A usage of larger fonts is to enhance messages, whether marketing or informational. By adding a weight of presence on the page, you can aid the observation and digestion of information. When combined with elements that have meaning—such as the strong element which exists to highlight important information—using a larger font provides both meaning in HTML content and an additional extra visual element to the text.

```
1.  <h1>Sizing and importance</h1>
2.     <p>Have fun in our pool, but ensure you <strong class="fs-5">never run beside the pool</strong> this action <strong class="fs-4 text-danger">may result in death!</strong></p>
```

When rendered, the result looks like this.

Sizing and importance

Have fun in our pool, but ensure you **never run beside the pool** this action may result in death!

In addition to the sizing, we also added a colour factor to enhance the second part of the warning.

```
1.  <!doctype html>
2.  <html lang="en">
3.
4.  <head>
5.     <title>Sizing and importance</title>
6.     <meta charset="utf-8">
7.     <meta name="viewport" content="width=device-width, initial-scale=1">
8.     <link href="https://cdn.jsdelivr.net/npm/bootstrap@5.0.0-beta3/dist/css/bootstrap.min.css" rel="stylesheet" >
9.  </head>
10.
11. <body class="p-2">
12.    <h1>Sizing and importance</h1>
13.    <p>Have fun in our pool, but ensure you <strong class="fs-5">never run beside the pool</strong> this action <strong class="fs-4 text-danger">may result in death!</strong></p>
14.    <script src="https://cdn.jsdelivr.net/npm/bootstrap@5.0.0-beta3/dist/js/bootstrap.bundle.min.js"></script>
15. </body>
16. </html>
```

TEXT STYLES AND WEIGHT

Bootstrap offers several classes that style text differently.

- fw-bold
- fw-bolder
- fw-normal
- fw-light
- fw-lighter
- fst-italic
- fst-normal

The fw stands for font weight and refers to the thickness or thinness of a font. The fst stands for font style.

When rendered, each class looks like this:

Text Styles

Bold
The light gray box, lay in front of the fox.

Bolder
The light gray box, lay in front of the fox.

Normal
The light gray box, lay in front of the fox.

Light
The light gray box, lay in front of the fox.

Lighter
The light gray box, lay in front of the fox.

Italic
The light gray box, lay in front of the fox.

Normal font style
The light gray box, lay in front of the fox.

The font weight should never be used on its own. It should be used with other elements such as Strong, em, and other elements that convey a meaning. Ideally, we should stick to one weight when conveying important information unless one part of the information is more important than another. As there is no way of distinguishing between the level of importance in HTML, we can visually represent that using a thicker, bolder, and larger font.

For sales and marketing, you can style the text to break up the page to make it more visually interesting and help hold attention. However, these practices are purely ornamental, and parts of your community who rely on accessibility tools will not find any inferred meaning using these styles.

EXAMPLE 18

The following is an example of the fonts being used.

```html
1.    <h1 class="display-1">Text Styles</h1>
2.    <h2>Bold</h2>
3.    <p class="fw-bold">The light gray box, lay in front of the fox.</p>
4.    <h2>Bolder</h2>
5.    <p class="fw-bolder">The light gray box, lay in front of the fox.</p>
6.    <h2>Normal</h2>
7.    <p class="fw-normal">The light gray box, lay in front of the fox.</p>
8.    <h2>Light</h2>
9.    <p class="fw-light">The light gray box, lay in front of the fox.</p>
10.   <h2>Lighter</h2>
11.   <p class="fw-lighter">The light gray box, lay in front of the fox.</p>
12.   <h2>Italic</h2>
13.   <p class="fst-italic">The light gray box, lay in front of the fox.</p>
14.   <h2>Normal font style</h2>
15.   <p class="fst-normal">The light gray box, lay in front of the fox.</p>
16.
```

The code above demonstrates each of the font weights and styles that can be used. You should not use italics on its own because this is included with the EM element. It may confuse users if you style text as italics, so please avoid doing this.

```html
1.  <!doctype html>
2.  <html lang="en">
3.
4.  <head>
5.      <title>Text Styles</title>
6.      <meta charset="utf-8">
7.      <meta name="viewport" content="width=device-width, initial-scale=1">
8.      <link href="https://cdn.jsdelivr.net/npm/bootstrap@5.0.0-beta3/dist/css/bootstrap.min.css" rel="stylesheet" crossorigin="anonymous">
9.  </head>
10.
11. <body class="p-2">
12.     <h1 class="display-1">Text Styles</h1>
13.     <h2>Bold</h2>
14.     <p class="fw-bold">The light gray box, lay in front of the fox.</p>
15.     <h2>Bolder</h2>
16.     <p class="fw-bolder">The light gray box, lay in front of the fox.</p>
17.     <h2>Normal</h2>
18.     <p class="fw-normal">The light gray box, lay in front of the fox.</p>
19.     <h2>Light</h2>
20.     <p class="fw-light">The light gray box, lay in front of the fox.</p>
21.     <h2>Lighter</h2>
22.     <p class="fw-lighter">The light gray box, lay in front of the fox.</p>
23.     <h2>Italic</h2>
24.     <p class="fst-italic">The light gray box, lay in front of the fox.</p>
25.     <h2>Normal font style</h2>
26.     <p class="fst-normal">The light gray box, lay in front of the fox.</p>
27.     <script src="https://cdn.jsdelivr.net/npm/bootstrap@5.0.0-beta3/dist/js/bootstrap.bundle.min.js" crossorigin="anonymous"></script>
28. </body>
29. </html>
```

The lighter fonts can be used as a stylistic choice but may cause users who have bad eyesight to struggle when reading text. It's best to avoid it.

TEXT LINE-HEIGHT

Line height is also known as line spacing. It is a term used to describe the vertical distance between two lines in a paragraph. Line spacing is an important aspect to consider when designing your website. It can make a vast difference to the understanding and readability of your content.

Conventional wisdom is that a line spacing of around 1.3 times the height of text to 1.5 times the height of text is ideal. There's enough space for most users to be able to clearly distinguish between two lines of text.

Bootstrap 5 has three levels and three classes: line-height-base, line-height-sm and line-height-lg.

Line-height-sm provides just 1.25 times the height of the text; we don't recommend using this.

Line-height-base is default for Bootstrap and gives a height of 1.5 times the height of text.

Meanwhile, if you need extra spacing you can use line-height-lg which provides 2 times the height of the text.

In most situations a 2 times line height is excessive, remaining with base, which is the default and recommended in most situations.

EXAMPLE 19

```html
1.  <!doctype html>
2.  <html lang="en">
3.  
4.  <head>
5.      <title>Text Line Height</title>
6.      <meta charset="utf-8">
7.      <meta name="viewport" content="width=device-width, initial-scale=1">
8.      <link href="https://cdn.jsdelivr.net/npm/bootstrap@5.0.0-beta3/dist/css/bootstrap.min.css" rel="stylesheet" crossorigin="anonymous">
9.  </head>
10. 
11. <body class="p-2">
12.     <h1 class="display-1">Text Line Height</h1>
13.     <h2>No height</h2>
14.     <p class="lh-1">Lorem ipsum dolor sit amet, consectetur adipiscing elit. Suspendisse dapibus lobortis venenatis. Sed risus tortor, aliquet et odio et, auctor elementum massa. Vivamus tristique libero sit amet placerat posuere. Pellentesque a est scelerisque, aliquam est ut, rhoncus odio. Curabitur sed maximus erat. Nam vestibulum non tortor nec tristique. Nam fringilla rhoncus accumsan. Vestibulum ante ipsum primis in faucibus orci luctus et ultrices posuere cubilia curae; Aliquam congue, leo in fermentum venenatis, lorem nibh tincidunt ipsum, ut euismod turpis turpis varius odio. Nulla ullamcorper quis metus non bibendum. In at turpis nec tortor dictum pharetra quis id ante. Cras ut nisl sagittis, blandit est eu, tincidunt risus.</p>
15.     <h2>Small</h2>
16.     <p class="lh-small">Ut eget erat ac felis lacinia porta a id neque. Mauris sagittis efficitur orci non interdum. Nulla id augue mauris. Mauris in semper mi, tincidunt suscipit urna. Integer metus sapien, aliquet quis sem vel, rutrum aliquam orci. Duis ornare finibus diam a fermentum. Aenean interdum purus vel aliquam ullamcorper. Quisque maximus semper libero et convallis. Morbi tristique lobortis magna, vel varius quam gravida eu. Nunc pharetra leo nisl, eu convallis sapien viverra quis. Praesent semper, nunc in vehicula imperdiet, diam erat ullamcorper ipsum, facilisis faucibus ligula ipsum ut lorem. Fusce sagittis maximus orci in varius. Integer laoreet viverra tortor. Nulla iaculis ipsum in nulla pretium accumsan. Suspendisse quis magna auctor, sodales elit at, rutrum sem. Nullam sit amet orci tincidunt, ullamcorper mi eget, bibendum massa.</p>
17.     <h2>Base</h2>
18.     <p class="lh-base">Integer quis dignissim leo. Nunc tincidunt turpis leo, id hendrerit augue lacinia quis. Maecenas egestas odio turpis, nec rhoncus dolor consectetur eu. Curabitur ut rutrum tellus. In nisi diam, vestibulum eget est ut, ultricies euismod ante. Aenean sit amet odio pulvinar, ornare ante id, sagittis nisi. Phasellus luctus nisi eu nibh ornare bibendum. Ut porttitor rutrum tortor non pharetra. Nam eget ligula non urna cursus volutpat. Vivamus in risus lacinia, fermentum mi molestie, dictum sem. Suspendisse scelerisque maximus nisl, maximus ullamcorper ante vulputate vel. Aenean id purus metus. Maecenas sed mauris sagittis, pulvinar dolor interdum, laoreet ante. Praesent fermentum commodo elit, vel ullamcorper tortor sodales placerat. Curabitur ante mauris, elementum quis mattis eget, suscipit et nisi. Integer vitae dolor pellentesque, euismod lacus at, molestie ex.</p>
19.     <h2>Large</h2>
20.     <p class="lh-large">Nunc vitae tortor maximus, accumsan ante ac, auctor neque. Praesent in commodo enim. Ut id sapien lobortis, porttitor sapien ut, blandit nulla. Sed pharetra luctus faucibus. Nullam pellentesque fermentum neque vitae mattis. Vivamus scelerisque congue nibh vitae vulputate. Nunc accumsan, justo a porttitor tincidunt, nulla purus elementum risus, a interdum sapien enim nec mi. Pellentesque habitant morbi tristique senectus et netus et malesuada fames ac turpis egestas. Nullam non lectus luctus, ultrices libero eget, mattis elit. Morbi laoreet metus vitae tempor aliquam. Maecenas sit amet tellus elit. Cras commodo vel felis vel vehicula. Nullam ultrices imperdiet vulputate. Donec hendrerit egestas erat, et condimentum mauris ornare eget. Pellentesque tristique, magna venenatis maximus sollicitudin, odio quam tincidunt magna, vel aliquet ligula arcu a velit.</p>
21.     <script src="https://cdn.jsdelivr.net/npm/bootstrap@5.0.0-beta3/dist/js/bootstrap.bundle.min.js" crossorigin="anonymous"></script>
22. </body>
23. </html>
```

TEXT TRANSFORM

The usage of capitalisation or lowercase draws many opinions from many sources. The average English teacher will explain the rules of grammar, while a marketer will talk about the importance of grabbing someone's attention at all costs. Someone who works with users who have cognitive issues, like learning disorders, will explain that using all capital letters can affect their ability to read negatively.

This last point is probably the most important—we need to ensure that anyone who visits a website can fully understand it. Keeping language as simple as possible and using the standard rules of English, combined with base font sizes and line heights, dramatically improves the readability of your content.

Some even find that big bold capital headings distract from the content they came to consume.

The classes you need to capitalize font are:

- text-lowercase
- text-uppercase
- text-capitalise

You will notice in this book that all the cases are lower, because in programming you need to use the right case or it will not work. This is an example of using lowercase.

EXAMPLE 20

The use of the classes is relatively simple, and we've applied it to the three paragraphs in this example.

The text-lowercase will convert all text to lowercase.

The text-uppercase will convert all text to uppercase.

The text-capitalise will capitalise the first letter in a sentence.

```html
1. <!doctype html>
2. <html lang="en">
3.
4. <head>
5.     <title>Text Transform</title>
6.     <meta charset="utf-8">
7.     <meta name="viewport" content="width=device-width, initial-scale=1">
8.     <link href="https://cdn.jsdelivr.net/npm/bootstrap@5.0.0-beta3/dist/css/bootstrap.min.css" rel="stylesheet" crossorigin="anonymous">
9. </head>
10.
11. <body class="p-2">
12.     <h1 class="display-1">Text Transform</h1>
13.     <h2 class="text-lowercase">Lowercase</h2>
14.     <p class="text-lowercase">Lorem ipsum dolor sit amet, consectetur adipiscing elit. Suspendisse dapibus lobortis venenatis. Sed risus tortor, aliquet et odio et, auctor elementum massa. Vivamus tristique libero sit amet placerat posuere. Pellentesque a est scelerisque, aliquam est ut, rhoncus odio. Curabitur sed maximus erat. Nam vestibulum non tortor nec tristique. Nam fringilla rhoncus accumsan. Vestibulum ante ipsum primis in faucibus orci luctus et ultrices posuere cubilia curae; Aliquam congue, leo in fermentum venenatis, lorem nibh tincidunt ipsum, ut euismod turpis turpis varius odio. Nulla ullamcorper quis metus non bibendum. In at turpis nec tortor dictum pharetra quis id ante. Cras ut nisl sagittis, blandit est eu, tincidunt risus.</p>
15.     <h2 class="text-uppercase">Uppercase</h2>
16.     <p class="text-uppercase">Ut eget erat ac felis lacinia porta a id neque. Mauris sagittis efficitur orci non interdum. Nulla id augue mauris. Mauris in semper mi, tincidunt suscipit urna. Integer metus sapien, aliquet quis sem vel, rutrum aliquam orci. Duis ornare finibus diam a fermentum. Aenean interdum purus vel aliquam ullamcorper. Quisque maximus semper libero et convallis. Morbi tristique lobortis magna, vel varius quam gravida eu. Nunc pharetra leo nisl, eu convallis sapien viverra quis. Praesent semper, nunc in vehicula imperdiet, diam erat ullamcorper ipsum, facilisis faucibus ligula ipsum ut lorem. Fusce sagittis maximus orci in varius. Integer laoreet viverra tortor. Nulla iaculis ipsum in nulla pretium accumsan. Suspendisse quis magna auctor, sodales elit at, rutrum sem. Nullam sit amet orci tincidunt, ullamcorper mi eget, bibendum massa.</p>
17.     <h2 class="text-capitalize">capitalize</h2>
18.     <p class="text-capitalize">integer quis dignissim leo. Nunc tincidunt turpis leo, id hendrerit augue lacinia quis. Maecenas egestas odio turpis, nec rhoncus dolor consectetur eu. Curabitur ut rutrum tellus. In nisi diam, vestibulum eget est ut, ultricies euismod ante. Aenean sit amet odio pulvinar, ornare ante id, sagittis nisi. Phasellus luctus nisi eu nibh ornare bibendum. Ut porttitor rutrum tortor non pharetra. Nam eget ligula non urna cursus volutpat. Vivamus in risus lacinia, fermentum mi molestie, dictum sem. Suspendisse scelerisque maximus nisl, maximus ullamcorper ante vulputate vel. Aenean id purus metus. Maecenas sed mauris sagittis, pulvinar dolor interdum, laoreet ante. Praesent fermentum commodo elit, vel ullamcorper tortor sodales placerat. Curabitur ante mauris, elementum quis mattis eget, suscipit et nisi. Integer vitae dolor pellentesque, euismod lacus at, molestie ex.</p>
19.     <script src="https://cdn.jsdelivr.net/npm/bootstrap@5.0.0-beta3/dist/js/bootstrap.bundle.min.js" crossorigin="anonymous"></script>
20. </body>
21. </html>
```

UNDERLINE STRIKETHROUGH AND REMOVAL OF UNDERLINE.

We can decorate text using an <u>underline</u>, a line ~~straight through text~~ or remove the underline from a hyperlink to make it look like normal text.

Some use underline instead of em when emphasizing text; however, this isn't a great idea because many users will confuse the text for a hyperlink.

When you update a blog with new information due to a correction or a previously printed piece of false information you can use the strikethrough on the old text and provide an update to it. This practice is used by people who wish to be honest with their user base. By using a strikethrough you can demonstrate that they did previously read some information in the blog or article, but has since been stricken off and replaced with corrected information.

It is worth noting that the element STRIKE exists to do the same job, and you should use this instead of using the Bootstrap style. The class is useful for HTML 4.01 where strike didn't exist.

We use the text decoration removal on hyperlinks to remove the underline, so it looks like normal text. This practice is common when creating buttons or other UI elements. However, because Bootstrap has a btn class, there's no reason to use this style unless you are building something styled. Remember that most users recognise the blue text with an underline as a hyperlink and we should maintain that convention especially when it is buried in a large paragraph of text. Part of accessibility is that information should not be identified by colour alone, so it must be a blue link or coloured link with an underline.

EXAMPLE 21

We have an example below, underlined text, a strikethrough showing updated information and an information strikeout.

The classes used are:

- text-decoration-underline
- text-decoration-line-through
- text-decoration-none

```
1.  <!doctype html>
2.  <html lang="en">
3.
4.  <head>
5.      <title>Underline strikethrough and removal of underline</title>
6.      <meta charset="utf-8">
7.      <meta name="viewport" content="width=device-width, initial-scale=1">
8.      <link href="https://cdn.jsdelivr.net/npm/bootstrap@5.0.0-beta3/dist/css/bootstrap.min.css" rel="stylesheet" >
9.  </head>
10.
11. <body class="p-2">
12.     <h1 class="display-1">Underline strikethrough and removal of underline</h1>
13.     <h2>A underlined piece of text.</h2>
14.     <p>This is some underlined text <span class="text-decoration-underline"> as you can see</span> it looks like a hyperlink.</p>
15.     <h2>A paragraph with updated information.</h2>
16.     <p>The meeting will be held at <span class="text-decoration-line-through">10pm on 11th May</span> 11pm on 10th May please be there early.</p>
17.     <h2>A paragraph with updated information.</h2>
18.     <p>The meeting will be held at <strike>10pm on 11th May</strike> 11pm on 10th May please be there early.</p>
19.     <h2>A hyperlink with underline removed</h2>
20.     <p>To obtain the special offer click <a href="www.ctelearning.com" class="text-decoration-none">CT<sup>e</sup> Learning</a> and gain 10% off!</p>
21.
22.     <script src="https://cdn.jsdelivr.net/npm/bootstrap@5.0.0-beta3/dist/js/bootstrap.bundle.min.js"></script>
23. </body>
24. </html>
```

You will notice no visual difference between the strike element and the styling class.

LISTS

Lists are used every day for organising information. They are used in surprising places.

Lists are used for two purposes.

The first is to organise data and display it to the user. For these you just need to use the usual <ul> and <ol> elements. Bootstrap will automatically style these without the need for classes.

The second is to organise elements within the page. Lists of links are a common use for this. You can also list UI elements such as radio buttons, checkboxes, and others.

We use the class list-unstyled with the <ul> element to remove the bullet points you would otherwise have. This can be commonly used in footers where you want to list your website or social media links.

Then we have the class list-inline, which are used when making a list that appears on the same line as everything else. This is commonly used in the nav bar at the top of the website.

The list-unstyled class gets applied to a single group of list items.

The list-inline gets applied to a single group of list items, then list-inline-item gets applied to every <li> element within that group to ensure they appear on the same line.

Lists

Unstyled List

Twitter
LinkedIn
Facebook
YouTube

Unstyled List Checkbox

Option 1 ☐
Option 2 ☐
Option 3 ☐
Option 4 ☐

Inline List

Home   Services   About   Help

Normal

- Eggs
- Milk
- Bread
- Cheese

EXAMPLE 22

The example below shows the classes in use. We have four sections—unstyled list of social media links, unstyled list of checkboxes, an inline list of menu links and a normal unstyled list.

```html
1.  <!doctype html>
2.  <html lang="en">
3.
4.  <head>
5.      <title>Lists</title>
6.      <meta charset="utf-8">
7.      <meta name="viewport" content="width=device-width, initial-scale=1">
8.      <link href="https://cdn.jsdelivr.net/npm/bootstrap@5.0.0-beta3/dist/css/bootstrap.min.css" rel="stylesheet" >
9.  </head>
10.
11. <body class="p-2">
12.     <h1 class="display-1">Lists</h1>
13.     <h2>Unstyled List</h2>
14.     <ul class="list-unstyled">
15.         <li><a href="#">Twitter</a></li>
16.         <li><a href="#">LinkedIn</a></li>
17.         <li><a href="#">Facebook</a></li>
18.         <li><a href="#">YouTube</a></li>
19.     </ul>
20.     <h2>Unstyled List Checkbox</h2>
21.     <ul class="list-unstyled">
22.         <li><label>Option 1</label> <input type="checkbox"></li>
23.         <li><label>Option 2</label> <input type="checkbox"></li>
24.         <li><label>Option 3</label> <input type="checkbox"></li>
25.         <li><label>Option 4</label> <input type="checkbox"></li>
26.     </ul>
27.     <h2>Inline List</h2>
28.     <ul class="list-inline">
29.         <li class="list-inline-item"><a href="#">Home</a></li>
30.         <li class="list-inline-item"><a href="#">Services</a></li>
31.         <li class="list-inline-item"><a href="#">About</a></li>
32.         <li class="list-inline-item"><a href="#">Help</a></li>
33.     </ul>
34.     <h2>Normal</h2>
35.     <ul>
36.         <li>Eggs</li>
37.         <li>Milk</li>
38.         <li>Bread</li>
39.         <li>Cheese</li>
40.     </ul>
41.     <script src="https://cdn.jsdelivr.net/npm/bootstrap@5.0.0-beta3/dist/js/bootstrap.bundle.min.js"></script>
42. </body></html>
```

BOOTSTRAP COLOURS

Colours can be added to Bootstrap using CSS and writing your own classes. Bootstrap comes with a series of predefined colours that convey specific meanings. The reason for doing this is that a standard is set and people can identify different information using colour.

We should never indicate information using colour alone, because there are colourblind users out there who can not perceive parts of the spectrum. However, we typically use these colours for everyone else to convey a meaning.

The following colour names are part of Bootstrap.

- Primary
- Secondary
- Success
- Danger
- Warning
- Info
- Dark
- Light

The primary colour blue conveys its presence through colour and is typically used on buttons and UI elements that perform an action.

Secondary colours are more muted and less obvious and are used on secondary UI elements.

Success colours indicate that a positive action has taken place. For example, a message stating that a mail has gone through, or an action has taken place.

A warning colour indicates that something has happened that might cause a problem. Maybe a mail didn't go through properly, or a warning message that a piece of data has not been entered into a form correctly.

The danger colour is for critical errors, critical issues and critical information such as health and safety notices. It can be as simple as a mail failed to send a message. Or a notice warning that a certain action will cause personal injury.

The info colour is designed to indicate a piece of information—for example, a help button might use it. Or a notice can be displayed explaining something.

Dark and Light are used to colour text and backgrounds for large contrasts. They are typically used as background and foreground colours.

Find an image indicating the colours.

Bootstrap Colours

Standard Colours

Primary	Secondary	Success
Danger	Warning	Info
Dark	Light	

Colours can be applied using the bg-* and text-* border-* class groups. You can use any of the named colours as either a background or foreground colour.

EXAMPLE 23

The example below produces the graphic we see above. We assign the colours to the bg-* class so the name indicated is the name of the background, not the foreground colour.

```html
1.  <!doctype html>
2.  <html lang="en">
3.
4.  <head>
5.      <title>Bootstrap Colours</title>
6.      <meta charset="utf-8">
7.      <meta name="viewport" content="width=device-width, initial-scale=1">
8.      <link href="https://cdn.jsdelivr.net/npm/bootstrap@5.0.0-beta3/dist/css/bootstrap.min.css" rel="stylesheet" crossorigin="anonymous">
9.  </head>
10.
11. <body class="p-2">
12.     <h1 class="display-1">Bootstrap Colours</h1>
13.     <h2>Standard Colours</h2>
14.     <div class="row">
15.         <div class="col-sm-4 bg-primary text-light">
16.             <p>Primary</p>
17.         </div>
18.         <div class="col-sm-4 bg-secondary text-light">
19.             <p>Secondary</p>
20.         </div>
21.         <div class="col-sm-4 bg-success text-light">
22.             <p>Success</p>
23.         </div>
24.     </div>
25.     <div class="row">
26.         <div class="col-sm-4 bg-danger text-light">
27.             <p>Danger</p>
28.         </div>
29.         <div class="col-sm-4 bg-warning text-dark">
30.             <p>Warning</p>
31.         </div>
32.         <div class="col-sm-4 bg-info text-dark">
33.             <p>Info</p>
34.         </div>
35.     </div>
36.     <div class="row">
37.         <div class="col-sm-6 bg-dark text-light">
38.             <p>Dark</p>
39.         </div>
40.         <div class="col-sm-6 bg-light text-dark">
41.             <p>Light</p>
42.         </div>
43.     </div>
44.     <script src="https://cdn.jsdelivr.net/npm/bootstrap@5.0.0-beta3/dist/js/bootstrap.bundle.min.js" crossorigin="anonymous"></script>
45. </body></html>
```

BORDERS

Every block element can have a border applied. The border is an outline of a block element. It is set all around using the class border.

Border will simply place a solid black line around a block element.

Border can be applied to the top, bottom, start and end of a block.

Borders are typically applied to highlight an important piece of information with a specific colour to help convey meaning—for example, error messages, information messages, success messages and others. The colour meaning applies to the meaning of the border as well.

For this we use the classes:

- border-top
- border-bottom
- border-start
- border-end

The start and end refer to left and right, in that order.

Additionally, we can apply colours to the border by adding the colour names:

- border-primary
- border-secondary
- border-success
- border-warning
- border-danger
- border-dark
- border-light
- border-info

Bootstrap border with colours

The primary colour full border

The secondary colour start border

The success colour end border

The warning colour bottom border

The danger colour top border

The info colour start and end border

The dark colour top and bottom border

The light colour top bottom start end border

EXAMPLE 24

The example below produces the image we see above. We use a combination of border, border-start, border-end and border-bottom classes. We combine it with the colours classes border-primary, border-secondary, border-success, etc.

```
1.  <!doctype html>
2.  <html lang="en">
3.  
4.  <head>
5.      <title>Bootstrap border with colours</title>
6.      <meta charset="utf-8">
7.      <meta name="viewport" content="width=device-width, initial-scale=1">
8.      <link href="https://cdn.jsdelivr.net/npm/bootstrap@5.0.0-beta3/dist/css/bootstrap.min.css" rel="stylesheet" >
9.  </head>
10. 
11. <body class="p-2">
12.     <h1>Bootstrap border with colours</h1>
13.     <div class="border border-primary m-2">The primary colour full border</div>
14.     <div class="border-start border-secondary m-2">The secondary colour start border</div>
15.     <div class="border-end border-success m-2">The success colour end border</div>
16.     <div class="border-bottom border-warning m-2">The warning colour bottom border</div>
17.     <div class="border-top border-danger m-2">The danger colour top border</div>
18.     <div class="border-start border-end border-info m-2">The info colour start and end border</div>
19.     <div class="border-bottom border-top border-dark m-2">The dark colour top and bottom border</div>
20.     <div class="border-end border-start border-top border-bottom border-light m-2">The light colour top bottom start end border</div>
21.     <script src="https://cdn.jsdelivr.net/npm/bootstrap@5.0.0-beta3/dist/js/bootstrap.bundle.min.js"></script>
22. </body></html>
```

EXAMPLE 25

In addition to creating border and assigning colours we can assign five levels of thickness with:

- border-1
- border-2
- border-3
- border-4
- border-5

Which you can see with the code below.

```
1.  <!doctype html>
2.  <html lang="en">
3.
4.  <head>
5.      <title>Bootstrap border thickness</title>
6.      <meta charset="utf-8">
7.      <meta name="viewport" content="width=device-width, initial-scale=1">
8.      <link href="https://cdn.jsdelivr.net/npm/bootstrap@5.0.0-beta3/dist/css/bootstrap.min.css" rel="stylesheet" >
9.  </head>
10.
11. <body class="p-2">
12.     <h1>Bootstrap border with colours</h1>
13.     <div class="border border-1 m-2">Border with thickness 1</div>
14.     <div class="border border-2 m-2">Border with thickness 2</div>
15.     <div class="border border-3 m-2">Border with thickness 3</div>
16.     <div class="border border-4 m-2">Border with thickness 4</div>
17.     <div class="border border-5 m-2">Border with thickness 5</div>
18.     <script src="https://cdn.jsdelivr.net/npm/bootstrap@5.0.0-beta3/dist/js/bootstrap.bundle.min.js"></script>
19. </body></html>
20.
```

The result looks like this:

Bootstrap border thickness

Border with thickness 1

Border with thickness 2

Border with thickness 3

Border with thickness 4

Border with thickness 5

MARGINS

Margins are the space around the border of a block element. The bigger the margin, the more space is assigned.

Margins can be used to bring attention to something important or separate blocks from one another.

Margins are called using the m-1, m-2, m-3, m-4, and m-5 classes. M-1 is the smallest margin and m-5 is the largest.

Bootstrap margins

Margin 1

Margin 2

Margin 3

Margin 4

Margin 5

EXAMPLE 26
Below we see simple margins set.

```
1.  <!doctype html>
2.  <html lang="en">
3.  
4.  <head>
5.      <title>Bootstrap margins</title>
6.      <meta charset="utf-8">
7.      <meta name="viewport" content="width=device-width, initial-scale=1">
8.      <link href="https://cdn.jsdelivr.net/npm/bootstrap@5.0.0-beta3/dist/css/bootstrap.min.css">
9.  </head>
10. 
11. <body class="p-2">
12.     <h1>Bootstrap margins</h1>
13.     <div class="border m-1">Border with thickness 1</div>
14.     <div class="border m-2">Border with thickness 2</div>
15.     <div class="border m-3">Border with thickness 3</div>
16.     <div class="border m-4">Border with thickness 4</div>
17.     <div class="border m-5">Border with thickness 5</div>
18.     <script src="https://cdn.jsdelivr.net/npm/bootstrap@5.0.0-beta3/dist/js/bootstrap.bundle.min.js"></script>
19. </body></html>
```

EXAMPLE 27

You can control the direction of the margin, assigning it to top, bottom, start and end as you do with borders.

Bootstrap margins

The margins below are set using the classes:

- m-*
- ms-*
- me-*
- my-*
- mx-*
- mt-*
- mb-*

They take sizing 1 to 5 as the previous set did.

The m-* class sets the complete margin border, the ms-* sets the left margin, me-* sets the right, mt-* sets top, mb-* sets bottom, mx-* sets both start and end at the same time while my-* sets the top and bottom at the same time.

```
1.  <!doctype html>
2.  <html lang="en">
3.
4.  <head>
5.      <title>Button Groups</title>
6.      <meta charset="utf-8">
7.      <meta name="viewport" content="width=device-width, initial-scale=1">
8.      <link href="https://cdn.jsdelivr.net/npm/bootstrap@5.0.0-beta3/dist/css/bootstrap.min.css" rel="stylesheet" crossorigin="anonymous">
9.  </head>
10.
11. <body class="p-2">
12.     <h1 class="display-1">Button Groups</h1>
13.     <div class="btn-group" role="group" aria-label="Basic example">
14.         <button type="button" class="btn btn-primary">Left</button>
15.         <button type="button" class="btn btn-success">Middle</button>
16.         <button type="button" class="btn btn-warning">Right</button>
17.     </div>
```

18.   `<script src="https://cdn.jsdelivr.net/npm/bootstrap@5.0.0-beta3/dist/js/bootstrap.bundle.min.js" crossorigin="anonymous"></script>`
19.   `</body></html>`

PADDING

Padding is the space between the border and the text, image, or of a block element.

Padding moves text and other elements like blocks, images, video, etc., away from the border of an element, even if the border is not visible. It stops text from being too close to border walls.

Margins are called using the p-1, p-2, p-3, p-4, and p-5 classes. The p-1 is the smallest margin and p-5 is the largest.

Bootstrap Padding

Padding 1

Padding 2

Padding 3

Padding 4

Padding 5

EXAMPLE 28
Below we see a simple padding set.

```html
1.  <!doctype html>
2.  <html lang="en">
3.
4.  <head>
5.      <title>Bootstrap Padding</title>
6.      <meta charset="utf-8">
7.      <meta name="viewport" content="width=device-width, initial-scale=1">
8.      <link href="https://cdn.jsdelivr.net/npm/bootstrap@5.0.0-beta3/dist/css/bootstrap.min.css" rel="stylesheet" integrity="sha384-eOJMYsd53ii+scO/bJGFsiCZc+5NDVN2yr8+0RDqr0Ql0h+rP48ckxlpbzKgwra6" crossorigin="anonymous">
9.  </head>
10.
11. <body class="p-2">
12.     <h1>Bootstrap Padding</h1>
13.     <div class="border p-1">Padding 1</div>
14.     <div class="border p-2">Padding 2</div>
15.     <div class="border p-3">Padding 3</div>
16.     <div class="border p-4">Padding 4</div>
17.     <div class="border p-5">Padding 5</div>
18.     <script src="https://cdn.jsdelivr.net/npm/bootstrap@5.0.0-beta3/dist/js/bootstrap.bundle.min.js" integrity="sha384-JEW9xMcG8R+pH31jmWH6WWP0WintQrMb4s7ZOdauHnUtxwoG2vI5DkLtS3qm9Ekf" crossorigin="anonymous"></script>
19. </body></html>
20.
```

EXAMPLE 29

You can control the direction of the padding, assigning it to top, bottom, start and end as you do with margins.

The margins below are set using the classes:

- m-*
- ms-*
- me-*
- my-*
- mx-*
- mt-*
- mb-*

They take sizing 1 to 5 as the previous set did.

The p-* class sets the complete padding border, the ps-* sets the left padding, pe-* sets the padding right, pt-* sets padding top, pb-* sets bottom, px-* sets both start and end at the same time while mpy-* sets the top and bottom at the same time.

```
1.  <!doctype html>
2.  <html lang="en">
3.
4.  <head>
5.      <title>Bootstrap padding direction</title>
6.      <meta charset="utf-8">
7.      <meta name="viewport" content="width=device-width, initial-scale=1">
8.      <link href="https://cdn.jsdelivr.net/npm/bootstrap@5.0.0-beta3/dist/css/bootstrap.min.css" rel="stylesheet">
9.  </head>
10.
11. <body class="p-2">
12.     <h1>Bootstrap padding</h1>
13.     <div class="border p-5">Padding all</div>
```

```
14.        <div class="border pt-5">Padding top</div>
15.        <div class="border pb-5">Padding bottom</div>
16.        <div class="border ps-5">Padding start</div>
17.        <div class="border pe-5">Padding end</div>
18.        <div class="border px-5">Padding X</div>
19.        <div class="border py-5">Padding Y</div>
20.        <script src="https://cdn.jsdelivr.net/npm/bootstrap@5.0.0-
beta3/dist/js/bootstrap.bundle.min.js"></script>
21. </body></html>
22.
```

BOOTSTRAP BUTTONS

Buttons are a very common UI element of Bootstrap, and their style can be used on hyperlinks, forms, dialog boxes and more.

Buttons can be created from multiple elements, including <a> <input> and <button>. Even <div> could be used, though it should only be used where the user is required to interact with that part of the website. Buttons handle colour changes when the mouse moves over them, and are visually set up so that the user knows that the text indicates an action will be taken—for example, the accepting of terms and conditions, the submission of an e-mail or a call to action where a user should click on a link.

The button is initially set up with the btn class, then a colour is assigned using the standard colour names.

- btn-primary
- btn-secondary
- btn-success
- btn-danger
- btn-warning
- btn-info
- btn-dark
- btn-light

The colour of the text inside the button is selected using the text-* class, which accepts the same standard Bootstrap colour names.

In addition to this we have btn-link, which makes the button look like a standard hyperlink—however, it is rarely used. The <a> element performs this action with the same styling, though it is not a block element.

EXAMPLE 30

The code below generates the buttons described above.

Buttons

[Primary] [Secondary] [Success] [Danger] [Warning] [Info] [Light] [Dark] [Link]

We simply create a button element and assign a class with btn and then btn-[colour].

```
1. <!doctype html>
2. <html lang="en">
3.
```

```html
4.  <head>
5.      <title>Buttons</title>
6.      <meta charset="utf-8">
7.      <meta name="viewport" content="width=device-width, initial-scale=1">
8.      <link href="https://cdn.jsdelivr.net/npm/bootstrap@5.0.0-beta3/dist/css/bootstrap.min.css" rel="stylesheet" crossorigin="anonymous">
9.  </head>
10.
11. <body class="p-2">
12.     <h1 class="display-1">Buttons</h1>
13.     <button type="button" class="btn btn-primary">Primary</button>
14.     <button type="button" class="btn btn-secondary">Secondary</button>
15.     <button type="button" class="btn btn-success">Success</button>
16.     <button type="button" class="btn btn-danger">Danger</button>
17.     <button type="button" class="btn btn-warning">Warning</button>
18.     <button type="button" class="btn btn-info">Info</button>
19.     <button type="button" class="btn btn-light">Light</button>
20.     <button type="button" class="btn btn-dark">Dark</button>
21.
22.     <button type="button" class="btn btn-link">Link</button>
23.     <script src="https://cdn.jsdelivr.net/npm/bootstrap@5.0.0-beta3/dist/js/bootstrap.bundle.min.js" crossorigin="anonymous"></script>
24. </body></html>
```

EXAMPLE 31

We can group buttons together so that they form a united panel. This is useful when we want controls or buttons presented as a choice rather than individual options.

Button Groups

The buttons are placed in a single div that is given the class btn-group, then the buttons are created as normal. Rather than being separated from one another, they appear side by side.

```
1.  <!doctype html>
2.  <html lang="en">
3.
4.  <head>
5.      <title>Button Groups</title>
6.      <meta charset="utf-8">
7.      <meta name="viewport" content="width=device-width, initial-scale=1">
8.      <link href="https://cdn.jsdelivr.net/npm/bootstrap@5.0.0-beta3/dist/css/bootstrap.min.css" rel="stylesheet" crossorigin="anonymous">
9.  </head>
10.
11. <body class="p-2">
12.     <h1 class="display-1">Button Groups</h1>
13.     <div class="btn-group" role="group" aria-label="Basic example">
14.         <button type="button" class="btn btn-primary">Left</button>
15.         <button type="button" class="btn btn-success">Middle</button>
16.         <button type="button" class="btn btn-warning">Right</button>
17.     </div>
18.     <script src="https://cdn.jsdelivr.net/npm/bootstrap@5.0.0-beta3/dist/js/bootstrap.bundle.min.js" crossorigin="anonymous"></script>
19. </body></html>
20.
```

BOOTSTRAP BUTTONS WITH OUTLINES

Buttons are a very common UI element of Bootstrap, and their style can be used on hyperlinks, forms, dialog boxes and more. In addition to normal buttons, you can create buttons with an outline style instead of a solid fill. There's no particular advantage to create outline buttons beyond styling.

Button Outlined

[Primary] [Secondary] [Success] [Danger] [Warning] [Info] [Dark]

Outline buttons can be created from multiple elements, including <a> <input> and <button>. Even <div> could be used, though it should only be used where the user is required to interact with that part of the website. Outline buttons handle colour changes when the mouse moves over them, and are visually set up so that the user knows that the text indicates an action will be taken—for example, the accepting of terms and conditions, the submission of an e-mail or a call to action where a user should click on a link.

The outline button is initially set up with the btn class, then a colour is assigned using the standard colour names.

- Btn-outline-primary
- Btn-outline-secondary
- Btn-outline-success
- Btn-outline-danger
- Btn-outline-warning
- Btn-outline-info
- Btn-outline-dark
- Btn-outline-light

The colour of the text inside the button is the same as the outline of the button. It can be changed independently but this would adjust the meaning of the button, so it is better to leave it consistent. A success border with a danger colour text, for example, would be very confusing.

EXAMPLE 32
The code below generates the buttons described above.

```html
1. <!doctype html>
2. <html lang="en">
3.
4. <head>
5.     <title>Button Outlined</title>
6.     <meta charset="utf-8">
7.     <meta name="viewport" content="width=device-width, initial-scale=1">
8.     <link href="https://cdn.jsdelivr.net/npm/bootstrap@5.0.0-beta3/dist/css/bootstrap.min.css" rel="stylesheet">
9. </head>
10.
11. <body class="p-2">
12.     <h1 class="display-1">Button Outlined</h1>
13.     <button type="button" class="btn btn-outline-primary">Primary</button>
14.     <button type="button" class="btn btn-outline-secondary">Secondary</button>
15.     <button type="button" class="btn btn-outline-success">Success</button>
16.     <button type="button" class="btn btn-outline-danger">Danger</button>
17.     <button type="button" class="btn btn-outline-warning">Warning</button>
18.     <button type="button" class="btn btn-outline-info">Info</button>
19.     <button type="button" class="btn btn-outline-light">Light</button>
20.     <button type="button" class="btn btn-outline-dark">Dark</button>
21.     <script src="https://cdn.jsdelivr.net/npm/bootstrap@5.0.0-beta3/dist/js/bootstrap.bundle.min.js"></script>
22. </body></html>
```

EXAMPLE 33

We can group buttons together so that they form a united panel. This is useful when we want controls or buttons presented as a choice rather than individual options.

Grouped Button Outlined

| Left | Middle | Right |

The buttons are placed in a single div that is given the class btn-group, then the buttons are created as normal. Rather than being separate from one another, they appear side by side.

```
1. <!doctype html>
2. <html lang="en">
3.
4. <head>
5.     <title>Grouped Button Outlined</title>
6.     <meta charset="utf-8">
7.     <meta name="viewport" content="width=device-width, initial-scale=1">
8.     <link href="https://cdn.jsdelivr.net/npm/bootstrap@5.0.0-beta3/dist/css/bootstrap.min.css" rel="stylesheet">
9. </head>
10.
11. <body class="p-2">
12.     <h1 class="display-1">Grouped Button Outlined</h1>
13.     <div class="btn-group" role="group" aria-label="Basic outlined example">
14.         <button type="button" class="btn btn-outline-primary">Left</button>
15.         <button type="button" class="btn btn-outline-success">Middle</button>
16.         <button type="button" class="btn btn-outline-danger">Right</button>
17.     </div>
18.     <script src="https://cdn.jsdelivr.net/npm/bootstrap@5.0.0-beta3/dist/js/bootstrap.bundle.min.js"></script>
19. </body></html>
```

END OF SECTION ACTIVITY

You've learned everything you need to create a fully featured web document, with heading styling, typography, colours, buttons and more.

Why not try making your very first website now?

You have everything you need to create beautiful blog posts, eBooks, articles, and more besides.

Imagine what you might use a website for and then sit down and write the content part of that site.

Here's some ideas to get you started:

- A florist article listing a range of stock.
- A blog post about your favourite topic.
- A personal online CV.
- A professional CV.
- Create memoirs or additional stories.

RESPONSIVE LAYOUT

This part of the book is dedicated to bootstrap layout, and design. Whitespace management, and everything it takes to create the block portions of your website.

Bootstrap is a mobile first responsive framework, everything in this section will allow you to create all the major components of a website. The nav, main portion and footer. With additional focus on managing cards, grids, columns, rows and more.

In this section you will learn:

- Website Layouts
- The Navigation Bar
- The Footer
- The Grid system.
- Containers and fluid containers.
- Rows.
- Columns
- Breakpoints.
- Whitespace management.
- Gutter control.

BOOTSTRAP CONTAINERS

Bootstrap containers are the most basic layout tool available to the framework. There are two types available, and their purpose is to contain and separate parts of your website or application.

The first type of container is referred to as the class *container*. it is required when using the Bootstrap grid system, which we will explore later. Containers are used to contain, pad, and align content.

The container class uses max-width breakpoints, a CSS rule that triggers upon a specific width.

Bootstrap is a popular open-source CSS framework used for developing responsive and mobile-first websites. In Bootstrap, the `.container` class is used to create a fixed-width, centered layout for a webpage. This is different from the `.container-fluid` class which creates a full-width container spanning the entire width of the viewport.

Here are some instances when a Bootstrap container is typically used in commercial website development:

Bootstrap's container class is primarily used when you want to center your site's content and provide horizontal padding to avoid touching the edge of the viewport. This gives your content a pleasant margin and a more polished look.

The container class gives you a responsive fixed width layout. The width adjusts at different predefined screen width points (known as breakpoints) based on the screen size. This is helpful when you want to limit the width of the content on larger screens.

Bootstrap's container class is also important when using the grid system, which allows up to 12 columns across the page. The container wraps these grid columns and ensures proper alignment and padding.

Websites that follow a conventional design pattern often make use of the Bootstrap container. Blogs, business websites, and educational sites are examples where the container class would be used to provide a structured and uniform layout.

When the content is text-heavy, like a blog or news website, it is often beneficial to limit the line length (number of characters on a line) to improve readability. The Bootstrap container class provides a way to easily manage this.

EXAMPLE 34

To assign a div, main or section element a container class, we use class="container".

The effect this class has is to centre content on standard desktop browser views with a width over 540px.

Bootstrap Container

The div below has container, and border classes attached.

100% wide until small breakpoint

The animation above shows a Browser Window being resized. The container snaps to the following pixel widths.

- 540px
- 720px
- 960px
- 1140px
- 1320px

Essentially, these are the widths that the container snaps too. Between snaps it centres the container to the browser viewport.

In addition to the container, we used border to add a visual outline to the container.

```
1.  <!doctype html>
2.  <html lang="en">
3.
4.  <head>
5.      <title>Bootstrap Container</title>
6.      <meta charset="utf-8">
7.      <meta name="viewport" content="width=device-width, initial-scale=1">
8.      <link href="https://cdn.jsdelivr.net/npm/bootstrap@5.0.0-beta3/dist/css/bootstrap.min.css" rel="stylesheet" crossorigin="anonymous">
9.  </head>
10.
11. <body>
12.
13.     <h1>Bootstrap Container</h1>
14.     <p>The div below has container, and border classes attached.</p>
15.
16.     <div class="container border">100% wide until small breakpoint</div>
17.
18.     <script src="https://cdn.jsdelivr.net/npm/bootstrap@5.0.0-beta3/dist/js/bootstrap.bundle.min.js" crossorigin="anonymous"></script>
19.
20. </body></html>
```

BOOTSTRAP CONTAINERS WITH BREAKPOINTS

In addition to the containers class we also have additional classes.

- container-sm
- container-md
- container-lg
- container-xl
- container-xxl

Sm stands for small, md stands for medium, lg stands for large, xl stands for extra large, and xxl stands for extra extra large.

The classes work in the same way as the normal container; however, the way they snap to resolutions is different.

Small is the same as just using a container, and it snaps between 540px to 1320px.

Medium doesn't start snapping until 720px.

Large snaps at 960px.

Extra Large snaps at 1140px.

Extra Extra Large snaps at 1320px.

Bootstrap Container with breakpoint

The div below has container, and border classes attached.

100% wide until small breakpoint
100% wide until small breakpoint
100% wide until medium breakpoint
100% wide until large breakpoint
100% wide until extra large breakpoint
100% wide until extra extra large breakpoint

The visualisation above demonstrates that the different breakpoints trigger based on the assigned values sm, md, lg, xl, and xxl. The xxl value snaps to a 100% width the soonest, whereas the sm value has the most sizes before it simply snaps to 100% width.

EXAMPLE 35

```html
1.  <!doctype html>
2.  <html lang="en">
3.
4.  <head>
5.      <title>Bootstrap Container with breakpoint</title>
6.      <meta charset="utf-8">
7.      <meta name="viewport" content="width=device-width, initial-scale=1">
8.      <link href="https://cdn.jsdelivr.net/npm/bootstrap@5.0.0-beta3/dist/css/bootstrap.min.css" rel="stylesheet" crossorigin="anonymous">
9.  </head>
10.
11. <body>
12.
13.     <h1>Bootstrap Container with breakpoint</h1>
14.     <p>The div below has container, and border classes attached.</p>
15.
16.     <div class="container border">100% wide until small breakpoint</div>
17.     <div class="container-sm border">100% wide until small breakpoint</div>
18.     <div class="container-md border">100% wide until medium breakpoint</div>
19.     <div class="container-lg border">100% wide until large breakpoint</div>
20.     <div class="container-xl border">100% wide until extra large breakpoint</div>
21.     <div class="container-xxl border">100% wide until extra extra large breakpoint</div>
22.
23.     <script src="https://cdn.jsdelivr.net/npm/bootstrap@5.0.0-beta3/dist/js/bootstrap.bundle.min.js" crossorigin="anonymous"></script>
24.
25. </body></html>
```

FLUID CONTAINER

The standard container snaps to pre-set pixel widths based on the size of the browser viewport.

The class *container-fluid,* however, adjusts to the browser viewport's size without snapping. Rather than centering the container and adjusting the size at breakpoints, the container fluidly resizes to the width of the body element.

In commercial website development, the fluid container class (typically named `.container-fluid` in frameworks such as Bootstrap) is used for creating layouts that scale and resize smoothly with the user's viewport. This is particularly important for ensuring that websites look good on a range of devices, from large desktop monitors to small mobile screens. Here are a few typical scenarios where a fluid container might be used:

Fluid containers are vital to creating responsive designs that adapt to different screen sizes. By using a fluid container, you ensure that the content will occupy the entire screen width, regardless of the viewport size.

If you're designing a website that requires full-width layouts (for instance, a landing page with full-width banners or images), a fluid container is the perfect choice. This ensures that the layout spans the entire width of the viewport, providing a seamless experience across different device types.

In combination with responsive grid systems, fluid containers allow developers to control how content reflows at different breakpoints. This enables more nuanced control over the layout across a variety of screen sizes.

If a website has dynamic data visualizations or charts that need to scale depending on the user's screen size, a fluid container could be used to ensure these elements resize appropriately.

For image galleries or sliders that should span the entire width of the screen, a fluid container can be beneficial. This ensures that the gallery will scale properly regardless of the user's viewport size.

Remember, while fluid containers are a powerful tool in responsive design, they should be used judiciously. For some content or design scenarios, a fixed-width container might be more appropriate to maintain the aesthetics or readability of the content.

EXAMPLE 36
Bootstrap Fluid Container

The div below has container, and border classes attached.

100% wide until small breakpoint
100% wide until small breakpoint
100% wide until medium breakpoint
100% wide until large breakpoint
100% wide until extra large breakpoint
100% wide until extra extra large breakpoint

100% wide with no breakpoints

The container is always 100% the width of the browser viewport.

```
1.  <!doctype html>
2.  <html lang="en">
3.
4.  <head>
5.      <title>Bootstrap Fluid Container</title>
6.      <meta charset="utf-8">
7.      <meta name="viewport" content="width=device-width, initial-scale=1">
8.      <link href="https://cdn.jsdelivr.net/npm/bootstrap@5.0.0-beta3/dist/css/bootstrap.min.css" rel="stylesheet" crossorigin="anonymous">
9.  </head>
10.
11. <body>
12.
13.     <h1>Bootstrap Fluid Container</h1>
14.     <p>The div below has container, and border classes attached.</p>
15.
16.     <div class="container border">100% wide until small breakpoint</div>
17.     <div class="container-sm border">100% wide until small breakpoint</div>
18.     <div class="container-md border">100% wide until medium breakpoint</div>
19.     <div class="container-lg border">100% wide until large breakpoint</div>
20.     <div class="container-xl border">100% wide until extra large breakpoint</div>
21.     <div class="container-xxl border">100% wide until extra extra large breakpoint</div>
22.     <div class="container-fluid border"><strong>100% wide with no breakpoints</strong></div>
23.
24.     <script src="https://cdn.jsdelivr.net/npm/bootstrap@5.0.0-beta3/dist/js/bootstrap.bundle.min.js" crossorigin="anonymous"></script>
25.
26. </body></html>
```

BOOTSTRAP GRID SYSTEM

The Bootstrap framework uses a grid system to create content layouts. A grid system uses rows and columns just as a table would.

Unlike a table you have a system where you can create as many rows as you like but are limited to twelve columns.

EXAMPLE 37

To create a row, we use the class *row*, and place it inside the class *container*.

```html
1.    <div class="container">
2.        <div class="row border">This is a row</div>
3.    </div>
```

The row acts as a container for a row of content. If you wish to have content that spans the width of the container, simply use a row, and place your content within it.

```html
1.  <!doctype html>
2.  <html lang="en">
3.
4.  <head>
5.      <title>Bootstrap Container and Row</title>
6.      <meta charset="utf-8">
7.      <meta name="viewport" content="width=device-width, initial-scale=1">
8.      <link href="https://cdn.jsdelivr.net/npm/bootstrap@5.0.0-beta3/dist/css/bootstrap.min.css" rel="stylesheet" crossorigin="anonymous">
9.  </head>
10.
11. <body>
12.
13.     <h1>Bootstrap Container and Row</h1>
14.     <p>The div below has container, and border classes attached.</p>
15.
16.     <div class="container">
17.         <span>This is the container. It controls the width of the elements inside.</span>
18.         <div class="row border">This is a row, this is a layout tool for stacking elements within a container.</div>
19.     </div>
20.
21.     <script src="https://cdn.jsdelivr.net/npm/bootstrap@5.0.0-beta3/dist/js/bootstrap.bundle.min.js" crossorigin="anonymous"></script>
22.
23. </body></html>
```

When we run the code, it then looks like this:

Bootstrap Container and Row

The div below has container, and border classes attached.

This is the container. It controls the width of the elements inside.
This is a row, this is a layout tool for stacking elements within a container.

A row will snap to the width of the container. If you use container-fluid it will extend across the entire width of the document.

EXAMPLE 38

If you wish to have several pieces of content side by side in the same row, use the class *col*.

Col will divide a row up to twelve times.

Let's start with a simple two column split.

To do this we just create two divs, both with col assigned.

```html
1. <!doctype html>
2. <html lang="en">
3.
4. <head>
5.     <title>Bootstrap Container and Row</title>
6.     <meta charset="utf-8">
7.     <meta name="viewport" content="width=device-width, initial-scale=1">
8.     <link href="https://cdn.jsdelivr.net/npm/bootstrap@5.0.0-beta3/dist/css/bootstrap.min.css" rel="stylesheet" crossorigin="anonymous">
9. </head>
10.
11. <body>
12.
13.     <h1>Bootstrap Container and Row</h1>
14.     <p>The div below has container, and border classes attached.</p>
15.
16.     <div class="container">
17.         <h2>This is the container</h2>
18.         <div class="row border">
19.             <h3>This is the row</h3>
20.             <div class="col border"><h4>This is the first column.</h4></div>
21.             <div class="col border"><h4>This is the second column</h4></div>
22.         </div>
23.     </div>
24.
25.     <script src="https://cdn.jsdelivr.net/npm/bootstrap@5.0.0-beta3/dist/js/bootstrap.bundle.min.js" crossorigin="anonymous"></script>
26.
27. </body></html>
```

With this code we get the following image.

Bootstrap Container and Row

The div below has container, and border classes attached.

This is the container
This is the row
This is the first column.   This is the second column

EXAMPLE 39

We can divide the row up to twelve times, but you cannot use the class border to add a visual presence. If you do, the columns will not fit all twelve.

Below is a visual demonstration of how each column reflows to fit your mobile device. As the screen becomes too narrow, the elements flow evenly onto new lines. Allowing your website to adjust accordingly. We have added a little colour so you can track the movement of the columns visually. Columns rearranging in this way is known as content reflowing.

Bootstrap Container and Row

The div below has container, and border classes attached.

This is the container

This is the row

| This is the first column. | This is the second column | This is the third column. | This is the forth column | This is the fifth column. | This is the sixth column | This is the seventh column. | This is the eighth column | This is the ninth column. | This is the tenth column | This is the eleventh column. | This is the twelth column |

COLUMN BREAKPOINTS

Columns will attempt to fit themselves as best as they can to the width of your browser viewport. Breakpoints allow layout designers to adjust columns for a mobile layout by defining at which point a column switch to 100% viewport width. We've seen this with container snapping too, where xxl will snap 100% width when below 1320px and small snaps below 540px.

The same principle applies when using column breakpoints.

This image demonstrates a normal reflow where no breakpoints have been set.

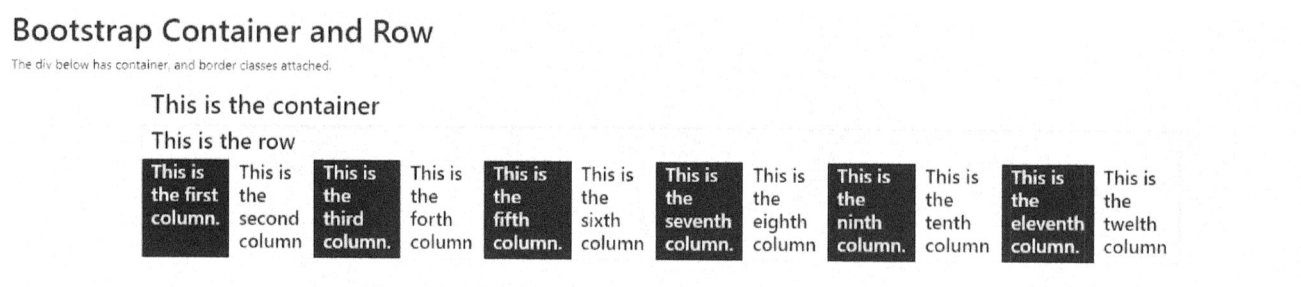

The following image demonstrates reflow, where the first six lines have received breakpoints xxl, xl, lg, md, and sm.

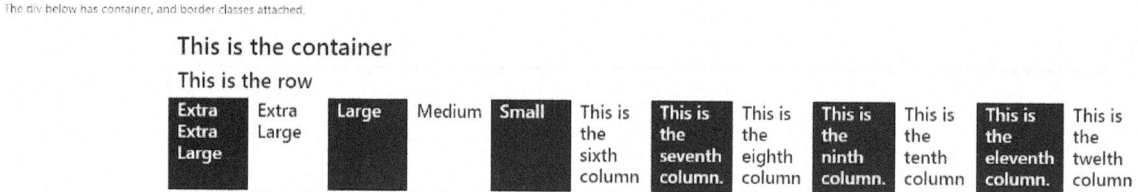

As the columns resize, the first to break to 100% is xxl, followed in order by xl, lg, md, and sm. The rest of the columns never leapt to 100%, but instead tried to divide the space between them evenly.

EXAMPLE 40

To add a breakpoint to a column, simply use the class col-* where the asterisk can be replaced with xxl, xl, lg, md and sm.

```html
1. <div class="col-xxl"><h4>Extra Extra Large</h4></div>
2. <div class="col-xl"><h4>Extra Large</h4></div>
3. <div class="col-lg"><h4>Large</h4></div>
4. <div class="col-md"><h4>Medium</h4></div>
5. <div class="col-sm"><h4>Small</h4></div>
```

COLUMN SIZING

When we use the col class, Bootstrap will evenly distribute the space between the columns. But we often want control over this spacing. To do this we can use a number range between one and twelve.

Because the maximum number of columns you can have per row is twelve, you can use that range of numbers.

To assign a width to a column, we use col-* where the asterisk can be replaced with any value between one and twelve.

EXAMPLE 41
The following example demonstrates multiple rows with different column configurations.

```html
1.  <!doctype html>
2.  <html lang="en">
3.  
4.  <head>
5.      <title>Bootstrap Column sizing</title>
6.      <meta charset="utf-8">
7.      <meta name="viewport" content="width=device-width, initial-scale=1">
8.      <link href="https://cdn.jsdelivr.net/npm/bootstrap@5.0.0-beta3/dist/css/bootstrap.min.css" rel="stylesheet" crossorigin="anonymous">
9.  </head>
10. 
11. <body>
12. 
13.     <h1>Bootstrap Column sizing</h1>
14.     <p>The div below has container, and border classes attached.</p>
15. 
16.     <div class="container">
17.         <h2>This is the container</h2>
18.         <div class="row">
19.             <h3>2 Columns automatic</h3>
20.             <div class="col"><div class="border"><h4>Column</h4></div></div>
21.             <div class="col"><div class="border"><h4>Column</h4></div></div>
22.         </div>
23.         <div class="row">
24.             <h3>2 Columns equal size</h3>
25.             <div class="col-6"><div class="border"><h4>Column width 6</h4></div></div>
26.             <div class="col-6"><div class="border"><h4>Column width 6</h4></div></div>
27.         </div>
28.         <div class="row">
29.             <h3>2 Columns uneven size</h3>
30.             <div class="col-10"><div class="border"><h4>Column width 10</h4></div></div>
31.             <div class="col-2"><div class="border"><h4>Column width 2</h4></div></div>
32.         </div>
33.         <div class="row">
34.             <h3>3 Columns 6-4-2 sizing</h3>
35.             <div class="col-6"><div class="border"><h4>Column width 6</h4></div></div>
36.             <div class="col-4"><div class="border"><h4>Column width 4</h4></div></div>
37.             <div class="col-2"><div class="border"><h4>Column width 2</h4></div></div>
38.         </div>
39.         <div class="row">
40.             <h3>3 Columns 2-6-4 sizing</h3>
41.             <div class="col-2"><div class="border"><h4>Column width 2</h4></div></div>
42.             <div class="col-6"><div class="border"><h4>Column width 6</h4></div></div>
43.             <div class="col-4"><div class="border"><h4>Column width 4</h4></div></div>
44.         </div>
45.         <div class="row">
46.             <h3>7 Columns 1-1-1-1-1-1-6 sizing</h3>
47.             <div class="col-1"><div class="border"><h4>Column width 1</h4></div></div>
48.             <div class="col-1"><div class="border"><h4>Column width 1</h4></div></div>
49.             <div class="col-1"><div class="border"><h4>Column width 1</h4></div></div>
50.             <div class="col-1"><div class="border"><h4>Column width 1</h4></div></div>
51.             <div class="col-1"><div class="border"><h4>Column width 1</h4></div></div>
52.             <div class="col-1"><div class="border"><h4>Column width 1</h4></div></div>
53.             <div class="col-6"><div class="border"><h4>Column width 6</h4></div></div>
54.         </div>
55.     </div>
56. 
57.     <script src="https://cdn.jsdelivr.net/npm/bootstrap@5.0.0-beta3/dist/js/bootstrap.bundle.min.js" crossorigin="anonymous"></script>
58. 
59. </body></html>
60. 
```

When tested, we have the following result.

Bootstrap Column sizing

The div below has container, and border classes attached.

This is the container

2 Columns automatic

| Column | Column |

2 Columns equal size

| Column width 6 | Column width 6 |

2 Columns uneven size

| Column width 10 | Column width 2 |

3 Columns 6-4-2 sizing

| Column width 6 | Column width 4 | Column width 2 |

3 Columns 2-6-4 sizing

| Column width 2 | Column width 6 | Column width 4 |

7 Columns 1-1-1-1-1-1-6 sizing

| Column width 1 | Column width 1 | Column width 1 | Column width 1 | Column width 1 | Column width 1 | Column width 6 |

Rather than having rows of equal spacing, we now have rows with different spacing configurations.

The first 2 Columns automatic and 2 Columns equal size achieve the same result using two different methods.

```
1. <h3>2 Columns automatic</h3>
2. <div class="col"><div class="border"><h4>Column</h4></div></div>
3. <div class="col"><div class="border"><h4>Column</h4></div></div>
```

The first uses the col class on it's own. The columns then automatically divide the space.

```
1. <h3>2 Columns equal size</h3>
2. <div class="col-6"><div class="border"><h4>Column width 6</h4></div></div>
3. <div class="col-6"><div class="border"><h4>Column width 6</h4></div></div>
```

Then we have col-6, which achieves the same result, but we manually define the size of each of the columns.

The result is:

2 Columns automatic

| Column | Column |

2 Columns equal size

| Column width 6 | Column width 6 |

Meanwhile, we can adjust the two columns so we have one wide and one short. We achieve this by setting column widths to ten and two. Remember that the total must be twelve when doing this or you will leave a space or go beyond the boundaries of the twelve columns.

```
1. <h3>2 Columns uneven size</h3>
2. <div class="col-10"><div class="border"><h4>Column width 10</h4></div></div>
3. <div class="col-2"><div class="border"><h4>Column width 2</h4></div></div>
```

The result looks like this:

This is the container

2 Columns automatic

| Column | Column |

2 Columns equal size

| Column width 6 | Column width 6 |

2 Columns uneven size

| Column width 10 | Column width 2 |

Column 10 is much wider than column 2.

You can have as many columns as you like, up to the value of twelve. However, at twelve there's no point in assigning values because it will have to divide equally to work. With eleven columns you can have one set to two, and the rest set to one. With six columns you can have a more varied range of sizes if they all calculate to twelve when added together.

Here's some three column examples that are very common when developing with Bootstrap.

They use a 6-4-2, 2-6-4, and there is a 7-column configuration set to 1-1-1-1-1-1-6.

```
1.  <div class="row">
2.      <h3>3 Columns 6-4-2 sizing</h3>
3.      <div class="col-6"><div class="border"><h4>Column width 6</h4></div></div>
4.      <div class="col-4"><div class="border"><h4>Column width 4</h4></div></div>
5.      <div class="col-2"><div class="border"><h4>Column width 2</h4></div></div>
6.  </div>
7.  <div class="row">
8.      <h3>3 Columns 2-6-4 sizing</h3>
9.      <div class="col-2"><div class="border"><h4>Column width 2</h4></div></div>
10.     <div class="col-6"><div class="border"><h4>Column width 6</h4></div></div>
11.     <div class="col-4"><div class="border"><h4>Column width 4</h4></div></div>
12. </div>
13. <div class="row">
14.     <h3>7 Columns 1-1-1-1-1-1-6 sizing</h3>
15.     <div class="col-1"><div class="border"><h4>Column width 1</h4></div></div>
16.     <div class="col-1"><div class="border"><h4>Column width 1</h4></div></div>
17.     <div class="col-1"><div class="border"><h4>Column width 1</h4></div></div>
18.     <div class="col-1"><div class="border"><h4>Column width 1</h4></div></div>
19.     <div class="col-1"><div class="border"><h4>Column width 1</h4></div></div>
20.     <div class="col-1"><div class="border"><h4>Column width 1</h4></div></div>
21.     <div class="col-6"><div class="border"><h4>Column width 6</h4></div></div>
22. </div>
```

The results look like this:

3 Columns 6-4-2 sizing

| Column width 6 | Column width 4 | Column width 2 |

3 Columns 2-6-4 sizing

| Column width 2 | Column width 6 | Column width 4 |

7 Columns 1-1-1-1-1-1-6 sizing

| Column width 1 | Column width 1 | Column width 1 | Column width 1 | Column width 1 | Column width 1 | Column width 6 |

COLUMN SIZING AND BREAKPOINTS

It is best to use column sizing and breakpoints together. If you use columns or column sizing on their own, the columns will divide the browser viewport width up evenly. The problem with this is that you can end up with some very messy mobile views.

Bootstrap Column sizing

The div below has container, and border classes attached.

This is the container

2 Columns automatic

| Column | Column |

2 Columns equal size

| Column width 6 | Column width 6 |

2 Columns uneven size

| Column width 10 | Column width 2 |

3 Columns 6-4-2 sizing

| Column width 6 | Column width 4 | Column width 2 |

3 Columns 2-6-4 sizing

| Column width 2 | Column width 6 | Column width 4 |

7 Columns 1-1-1-1-1-1-6 sizing

| Column width 1 | Column width 1 | Column width 1 | Column width 1 | Column width 1 | Column width 1 | Column width 6 |

You will notice that at minimum width the content flows outside boxes, overlaps and generally creates an ugly mobile website.

If we add breakpoints to the setup, we end up with a much more pleasant layout.

Bootstrap Column sizing

The div below has container, and border classes attached.

This is the container

2 Columns automatic

| Column | Column |

2 Columns equal size

| Column width 6 | Column width 6 |

2 Columns uneven size

| Column width 10 | Column width 2 |

3 Columns 6-4-2 sizing

| Column width 6 | Column width 4 | Column width 2 |

3 Columns 2-6-4 sizing

| Column width 2 | Column width 6 | Column width 4 |

7 Columns 1-1-1-1-1-1-6 sizing

| Column width 1 | Column width 1 | Column width 1 | Column width 1 | Column width 1 | Column width 1 | Column width 6 |

When the breakpoints are reached they automatically reflow to the full width of the display, creating a stacked mobile layout.

We use the col-sm-*, col-md-*, col-lg-*, col-xl-*, col-xxl-* classes to set the breakpoints and then set the width by replacing the asterisk with a value between one and twelve.

The result is a website that uses these columns.

EXAMPLE 42

```html
1.  <!doctype html>
2.  <html lang="en">
3.  
4.  <head>
5.      <title>Bootstrap Column sizing</title>
6.      <meta charset="utf-8">
7.      <meta name="viewport" content="width=device-width, initial-scale=1">
8.      <link href="https://cdn.jsdelivr.net/npm/bootstrap@5.0.0-beta3/dist/css/bootstrap.min.css" rel="stylesheet" crossorigin="anonymous">
9.  </head>
10. 
11. <body>
12. 
13.     <h1>Bootstrap Column sizing</h1>
14.     <p>The div below has container, and border classes attached.</p>
15. 
16.     <div class="container">
17.         <h2>This is the container</h2>
18.         <div class="row">
19.             <h3>2 Columns automatic</h3>
20.             <div class="col"><div class="border"><h4>Column</h4></div></div>
21.             <div class="col"><div class="border"><h4>Column</h4></div></div>
22.         </div>
23.         <div class="row">
24.             <h3>2 Columns equal size</h3>
25.             <div class="col-lg-6"><div class="border"><h4>Column width 6</h4></div></div>
26.             <div class="col-lg-6"><div class="border"><h4>Column width 6</h4></div></div>
27.         </div>
28.         <div class="row">
29.             <h3>2 Columns uneven size</h3>
30.             <div class="col-xxl-10"><div class="border"><h4>Column width 10</h4></div></div>
31.             <div class="col-md-2"><div class="border"><h4>Column width 2</h4></div></div>
32.         </div>
33.         <div class="row">
34.             <h3>3 Columns 6-4-2 sizing</h3>
35.             <div class="col-lg-6"><div class="border"><h4>Column width 6</h4></div></div>
36.             <div class="col-md-4"><div class="border"><h4>Column width 4</h4></div></div>
37.             <div class="col-md-2"><div class="border"><h4>Column width 2</h4></div></div>
38.         </div>
39.         <div class="row">
40.             <h3>3 Columns 2-6-4 sizing</h3>
41.             <div class="col-lg-2"><div class="border"><h4>Column width 2</h4></div></div>
42.             <div class="col-lg-6"><div class="border"><h4>Column width 6</h4></div></div>
43.             <div class="col-lg-4"><div class="border"><h4>Column width 4</h4></div></div>
44.         </div>
45.         <div class="row">
46.             <h3>7 Columns 1-1-1-1-1-1-6 sizing</h3>
47.             <div class="col-xl-1"><div class="border"><h4>Column width 1</h4></div></div>
48.             <div class="col-xl-1"><div class="border"><h4>Column width 1</h4></div></div>
49.             <div class="col-xl-1"><div class="border"><h4>Column width 1</h4></div></div>
50.             <div class="col-xl-1"><div class="border"><h4>Column width 1</h4></div></div>
51.             <div class="col-xl-1"><div class="border"><h4>Column width 1</h4></div></div>
52.             <div class="col-xl-1"><div class="border"><h4>Column width 1</h4></div></div>
53.             <div class="col-xl-6"><div class="border"><h4>Column width 6</h4></div></div>
54.         </div>
55.     </div>
56. 
57.     <script src="https://cdn.jsdelivr.net/npm/bootstrap@5.0.0-beta3/dist/js/bootstrap.bundle.min.js" crossorigin="anonymous"></script>
58. 
59. </body></html>
```

By adding breakpoints through carefully observing if content goes outside of their columns we create a truly responsive design that will work on anything.

IMAGES

Images are controlled and styled with the following classes.

- w-100
- w-75
- w-50
- w-25
- img-fluid
- img-thumbnail
- float-start
- float-end
- mx-auto

The w series classes set the width of the image. They are percentage based, so 100 is full width, 75 is three quarters or 75%, 50 is half or 50%, and 25 is one quarter or 25% width. They take their width from the parent container, so if you place it in a row or column it will take the percentage of the div element it is placed in.

The img-fluid class works in the same way as w-100—it simply scales the image to 100% of the container width.

The img-thumbnail class provides a border around the image indicating that it is a thumbnail of a larger image. This is often combined with modals, which pop-up when the image is clicked and show the full image.

The float-start class takes the image out of the normal flow. It will not work inside a row or column class, only a container. The float-end does the same except it aligns the image with the right side of the screen.

The mx-auto sets automatic margins on the left and right of the image, allowing you to centre it.

EXAMPLE 43

Below we have code that shows the images in their various positions, sizes, and styles.

```html
1.  <!doctype html>
2.  <html lang="en">
3.
4.  <head>
5.      <title>Image sizing and alignment</title>
6.      <meta charset="utf-8">
7.      <meta name="viewport" content="width=device-width, initial-scale=1">
8.      <link href="https://cdn.jsdelivr.net/npm/bootstrap@5.0.0-beta3/dist/css/bootstrap.min.css" rel="stylesheet">
9.  </head>
10.
11. <body class="p-2">
12.     <h1>Image sizing and alignment</h1>
13.     <div class="container-fluid">
14.         <div class="row m-2">
15.             <img src="https://via.placeholder.com/1000x250?text=Full+Width" class="w-100">
16.         </div>
17.         <div class="row m-2">
18.             <img src="https://via.placeholder.com/1000x250?text=Three+Quaters+Width" class="w-75">
19.         </div>
20.         <div class="row m-2">
21.             <img src="https://via.placeholder.com/1000x250?text=Half+Width" class="w-50">
22.         </div>
23.         <div class="row m-2">
24.             <img src="https://via.placeholder.com/1000x250?text=Quater+Width" class="w-25">
25.         </div>
26.         <div class="row m-2">
27.             <img src="https://via.placeholder.com/1000x250?text=Fluid+Image" class="img-fluid">
28.         </div>
29.         <div class="row m-2">
30.             <img src="https://via.placeholder.com/500x500?text=Image+thumbnail" class="img-thumbnail w-50">
31.         </div>
32.         <div class="row m-2">
33.             <img src="https://via.placeholder.com/250x250?text=Centered+Image" class="w-25 mx-auto">
34.         </div>
35.         <img src="https://via.placeholder.com/250x250?text=Float+Start" class="w-25 float-start">
36.         <img src="https://via.placeholder.com/250x250?text=Float+End" class="w-25 float-end">
37.     </div>
38.
39.     <script src="https://cdn.jsdelivr.net/npm/bootstrap@5.0.0-beta3/dist/js/bootstrap.bundle.min.js">
40.     </script>
41. </body>
42.
43. </html>
```

CARDS

Cards are a UI (User Interface) item and are somewhat inspired by their real-life counterparts. A card is a UI container that holds a few pieces of related information. They roughly represent the playing card in shape and size. They are presentation units.

The vast majority of website designs work around cards because they work well with responsive web design. As you scale the browser down, the cards "resize" and "reshuffle" their position on the user's screen.

Three cards side by side:

Three cards stacked for a mobile display:

Each card is a single card class, which is then further divided into three parts in the same way a website is.

- Card Header
- Card Body
- Card Footer

The header of the card is made up of an image or a title. The example we're going to use is one with an image that is the most visually striking. If you use an image header you can move the heading into the card body and write it as a single article of text.

Then we have the card body, which contains the single article of text.

Finally, we have the card footer, which can hold a summary of the card, details of the author, a call-to-action button, social media links or links to a larger full page article if you're previewing content elsewhere on the site.

Cards are made up of the following class structure:

- card
    - card-header
        - card-img-top
    - card-body
        - card-title
        - card-text
    - card-footer
        - btn btn-primary

```html
1.  <div class="card">
2.      <div class="card-header p-0">
3.          <img src="https://via.placeholder.com/350x150" class="card-img-top" alt="placeholder image">
4.      </div>
5.      <div class="card-body p-2">
6.          <h2 class="card-title">Card title</h2>
7.          <p class="card-text">Lorem ipsum dolor sit amet, consectetur adipiscing elit. Aliquam a semper urna. Pellentesque at massa metus. Vivamus justo augue, accumsan sit amet odio ut, sollicitudin rhoncus leo. Fusce non felis non mi fringilla tincidunt ac in arcu. Fusce elit justo, hendrerit eget augue a, suscipit luctus urna. Aenean eu neque pulvinar, pharetra mauris at, facilisis est. Fusce eu commodo quam, eu rhoncus tellus. Duis nec eros elit.</p>
8.      </div>
9.      <div class="card-footer">
10.         <a href="#" class="btn btn-primary">Call to action</a>
11.     </div>
12. </div>
```

To help style the card so it looks nice, we add a p-0 to the card-header, and a p-2 to the card body.

EXAMPLE 44

In this example we demonstrate a pair of cards sitting comfortably side by side. As the display resizes, they stack on top of each other. The breakpoints and layouts are all controlled by the column techniques you learned previously. This means you could have up to 12 cards side by side, but four is the more normal maximum.

```
1.  <!doctype html>
2.  <html lang="en">
3.
4.  <head>
5.      <title>Basic Cards</title>
6.      <meta charset="utf-8">
7.      <meta name="viewport" content="width=device-width, initial-scale=1">
8.      <link href="https://cdn.jsdelivr.net/npm/bootstrap@5.0.0-beta3/dist/css/bootstrap.min.css" rel="stylesheet"
9.          crossorigin="anonymous">
10. </head>
11.
12. <body>
13.
14.     <h1>Basic Cards</h1>
15.     <p>Find a basic card setup below.</p>
16.
17.     <div class="container">
18.         <div class="row">
19.             <div class="col-md-6 mb-2">
20.                 <div class="card">
21.                     <img src="https://via.placeholder.com/350x150" class="card-img-top" alt="placeholder image">
22.                     <div class="card-body">
23.                         <h2 class="card-title">Card title</h2>
24.                         <p class="card-text">Lorem ipsum dolor sit amet, consectetur adipiscing elit. Aliquam a semper urna. Pellentesque at massa metus. Vivamus justo augue, accumsan sit amet odio ut, sollicitudin rhoncus leo. Fusce non felis non mi fringilla tincidunt ac in arcu. Fusce elit justo, hendrerit eget augue a, suscipit luctus urna. Aenean eu neque pulvinar, pharetra mauris at, facilisis est. Fusce eu commodo quam, eu rhoncus tellus. Duis nec eros elit.</p>
25.                         <a href="#" class="btn btn-primary">Go somewhere</a>
26.                     </div>
27.                     <div class="card-footer">
28.                         Card footer
29.                     </div>
30.                 </div>
31.             </div>
32.             <div class="col-md-6 mb-2">
33.                 <div class="card">
34.                     <img src="https://via.placeholder.com/350x150" class="card-img-top" alt="placeholder image">
35.                     <div class="card-body">
36.                         <h2 class="card-title">Card title</h2>
37.                         <p class="card-text">Lorem ipsum dolor sit amet, consectetur adipiscing elit. Aliquam a semper urna. Pellentesque at massa metus. Vivamus justo augue, accumsan sit amet odio ut, sollicitudin rhoncus leo. Fusce non felis non mi fringilla tincidunt ac in arcu. Fusce elit justo, hendrerit eget augue a, suscipit luctus urna. Aenean eu neque pulvinar, pharetra mauris at, facilisis est. Fusce eu commodo quam, eu rhoncus tellus. Duis nec eros elit.</p>
38.                         <a href="#" class="btn btn-primary">Go somewhere</a>
39.                     </div>
40.                     <div class="card-footer">
41.                         Card footer
42.                     </div>
43.                 </div>
44.             </div>
45.         </div>
46.     </div>
47.
48.     <script src="https://cdn.jsdelivr.net/npm/bootstrap@5.0.0-beta3/dist/js/bootstrap.bundle.min.js"
49.         crossorigin="anonymous"></script>
```

```
50. 
51. </body>
52. 
53. </html>
```

GUTTERS

Gutters represent the spacing between your columns. They are used to space and align content in the Bootstrap grid system. Many inexperienced users will attempt to use margins and padding to create the spaces they want between their columns; however, this will mess up the layout of the cards. To add both horizontal and vertical spacing we use the gutter classes.

Horizontal spacing is achieved using the gx-* class, which accepts values up to 5. The higher the value, the wider the spacing between columns.

For vertical spacing we use the gy-* class, which also accepts values up to 5. Again, the higher the value, the wider the spacing between the top and bottom of rows.

The gx-* and gy-* classes are applied to the element with a row class, and the gutter sizing is then carried on throughout the column structure.

EXAMPLE 45
The example below shows horizontal gutter sizing.

Bootstrap Horizontal Gutter Sizing

The container below, has rows with a horizontal gutter applied at varied levels.

Column with gutter of 1	Column with gutter of 1
Column with gutter of 2	Column with gutter of 2
Column with gutter of 3	Column with gutter of 3
Column with gutter of 4	Column with gutter of 4
Column with gutter of 5	Column with gutter of 5

As you can see, in this simple two column design we have ever-increasing spacing between the columns, which is carried on for all the columns.

Look for the row classes and you will see that a gx-* has been applied, which then carries on throughout the whole row classed element.

```
1.  <!doctype html>
2.  <html lang="en">
3.
4.  <head>
5.      <title>Bootstrap Horizontal Gutter Sizing</title>
6.      <meta charset="utf-8">
7.      <meta name="viewport" content="width=device-width, initial-scale=1">
8.      <link href="https://cdn.jsdelivr.net/npm/bootstrap@5.0.0-beta3/dist/css/bootstrap.min.css" rel="stylesheet"
9.          crossorigin="anonymous">
10. </head>
11.
12. <body>
13.
14.     <h1>Bootstrap Horizontal Gutter Sizing</h1>
15.     <p>The container below, has rows with a horizontal gutter applied at varied levels.</p>
16.
17.     <div class="container">
18.         <div class="row gx-1">
19.             <div class="col">
20.                 <div class="p-3 border bg-light">Column with gutter of 1</div>
21.             </div>
22.             <div class="col">
23.                 <div class="p-3 border bg-light">Column with gutter of 1</div>
24.             </div>
25.         </div>
26.         <div class="row gx-2">
27.             <div class="col">
28.                 <div class="p-3 border bg-light">Column with gutter of 2</div>
29.             </div>
30.             <div class="col">
31.                 <div class="p-3 border bg-light">Column with gutter of 2</div>
32.             </div>
33.         </div>
34.         <div class="row gx-3">
35.             <div class="col">
36.                 <div class="p-3 border bg-light">Column with gutter of 3</div>
```

```html
37.            </div>
38.            <div class="col">
39.                <div class="p-3 border bg-light">Column with gutter of 3</div>
40.            </div>
41.        </div>
42.        <div class="row gx-4">
43.            <div class="col">
44.                <div class="p-3 border bg-light">Column with gutter of 4</div>
45.            </div>
46.            <div class="col">
47.                <div class="p-3 border bg-light">Column with gutter of 4</div>
48.            </div>
49.        </div>
50.        <div class="row gx-5">
51.            <div class="col">
52.                <div class="p-3 border bg-light">Column with gutter of 5</div>
53.            </div>
54.            <div class="col">
55.                <div class="p-3 border bg-light">Column with gutter of 5</div>
56.            </div>
57.        </div>
58.    </div>
59.
60.    <script src="https://cdn.jsdelivr.net/npm/bootstrap@5.0.0-beta3/dist/js/bootstrap.bundle.min.js"
61.        crossorigin="anonymous"></script>
62.
63. </body>
64.
65. </html>
66.
```

EXAMPLE 46

Next, we apply the gy-* class to the div element that has the class rows assigned. By doing this, the columns are affected automatically within that div. The gutter spacing will increase with each instance of this action.

Look for the row and gy-* values to see the comparison.

```
1.  <!doctype html>
2.  <html lang="en">
3.
4.  <head>
5.      <title>Bootstrap Vertical Gutter Sizing</title>
6.      <meta charset="utf-8">
7.      <meta name="viewport" content="width=device-width, initial-scale=1">
8.      <link href="https://cdn.jsdelivr.net/npm/bootstrap@5.0.0-beta3/dist/css/bootstrap.min.css" rel="stylesheet"
9.          crossorigin="anonymous">
10. </head>
11.
12. <body>
13.
14.     <h1>Bootstrap Vertical Gutter Sizing</h1>
15.     <p>The container below has rows with a vertical gutter applied at varied levels.</p>
16.
17.     <div class="container">
18.
19.         <div class="row gy-1 border my-3 pb-1">
20.             <div class="col-6">
21.                 <div class="p-3 border bg-light">Column 1</div>
22.             </div>
```

```html
23.            <div class="col-6">
24.                <div class="p-3 border bg-light">Column 2</div>
25.            </div>
26.            <div class="col-6">
27.                <div class="p-3 border bg-light">Column 3</div>
28.            </div>
29.            <div class="col-6">
30.                <div class="p-3 border bg-light">Column 4</div>
31.            </div>
32.        </div>
33.
34.        <div class="row gy-2 border my-3 pb-2">
35.            <div class="col-6">
36.                <div class="p-3 border bg-light">Column 1</div>
37.            </div>
38.            <div class="col-6">
39.                <div class="p-3 border bg-light">Column 2</div>
40.            </div>
41.            <div class="col-6">
42.                <div class="p-3 border bg-light">Column 3</div>
43.            </div>
44.            <div class="col-6">
45.                <div class="p-3 border bg-light">Column 4</div>
46.            </div>
47.        </div>
48.
49.        <div class="row gy-3 border my-3 pb-3">
50.            <div class="col-6">
51.                <div class="p-3 border bg-light">Column 1</div>
52.            </div>
53.            <div class="col-6">
54.                <div class="p-3 border bg-light">Column 2</div>
55.            </div>
56.            <div class="col-6">
57.                <div class="p-3 border bg-light">Column 3</div>
58.            </div>
59.            <div class="col-6">
60.                <div class="p-3 border bg-light">Column 4</div>
61.            </div>
62.        </div>
63.
64.        <div class="row gy-4 border my-3 pb-4">
65.            <div class="col-6">
66.                <div class="p-3 border bg-light">Column 1</div>
67.            </div>
68.            <div class="col-6">
69.                <div class="p-3 border bg-light">Column 2</div>
70.            </div>
71.            <div class="col-6">
72.                <div class="p-3 border bg-light">Column 3</div>
73.            </div>
74.            <div class="col-6">
75.                <div class="p-3 border bg-light">Column 4</div>
76.            </div>
77.        </div>
78.
79.        <div class="row gy-5 border my-3 pb-5">
80.            <div class="col-6">
81.                <div class="p-3 border bg-light">Column 1</div>
82.            </div>
83.            <div class="col-6">
84.                <div class="p-3 border bg-light">Column 2</div>
85.            </div>
86.            <div class="col-6">
87.                <div class="p-3 border bg-light">Column 3</div>
88.            </div>
89.            <div class="col-6">
90.                <div class="p-3 border bg-light">Column 4</div>
```

```html
91.            </div>
92.         </div>
93.
94.     </div>
95.
96.     <script src="https://cdn.jsdelivr.net/npm/bootstrap@5.0.0-beta3/dist/js/bootstrap.bundle.min.js"
97.         crossorigin="anonymous"></script>
98.
99. </body>
100.
101. </html>
```

EXAMPLE 47

Finally we have the gx-* and gy-* classes combine in ever-increasing values to create a very interesting and complicated website layout.

If you look at websites like YouTube, Netflix and others you will see a very similar style of layout.

Take the time to look at the way Amazon is laid out, and how Google organises photographs. You will see this responsive layout method used across the internet.

```
1.  <!doctype html>
2.  <html lang="en">
3.
4.  <head>
5.      <title>Bootstrap Horizontal Gutter Sizing</title>
6.      <meta charset="utf-8">
7.      <meta name="viewport" content="width=device-width, initial-scale=1">
8.      <link href="https://cdn.jsdelivr.net/npm/bootstrap@5.0.0-beta3/dist/css/bootstrap.min.css" rel="stylesheet">
9.  </head>
10.
11. <body>
12.
13.     <h1>Bootstrap Vertical Gutter Sizing</h1>
14.     <p>The container below, has rows with a vertical gutter applied at varied levels.</p>
15.
16.     <div class="container">
17.
18.         <h2>Size 1 on x and y gutter</h2>
19.
20.         <div class="row gx-1 gy-1">
21.             <div class="col">
22.                 <div class="p-3 border">Column</div>
23.             </div>
24.             <div class="col">
25.                 <div class="p-3 border">Column</div>
26.             </div>
27.             <div class="col">
```

```html
            <div class="p-3 border">Column</div>
        </div>
        <div class="col">
            <div class="p-3 border">Column</div>
        </div>
        <div class="col">
            <div class="p-3 border">Column</div>
        </div>
        <div class="col">
            <div class="p-3 border">Column</div>
        </div>
        <div class="col">
            <div class="p-3 border">Column</div>
        </div>
        <div class="col">
            <div class="p-3 border">Column</div>
        </div>
        <div class="col">
            <div class="p-3 border">Column</div>
        </div>
        <div class="col">
            <div class="p-3 border">Column</div>
        </div>
    </div>

</div>

<div class="container mt-2">

    <h2>Size 3 on x and y gutter</h2>

    <div class="row gx-3 gy-3">
        <div class="col">
            <div class="p-3 border">Column</div>
        </div>
        <div class="col">
            <div class="p-3 border">Column</div>
        </div>
        <div class="col">
            <div class="p-3 border">Column</div>
        </div>
        <div class="col">
            <div class="p-3 border">Column</div>
        </div>
        <div class="col">
            <div class="p-3 border">Column</div>
        </div>
        <div class="col">
            <div class="p-3 border">Column</div>
        </div>
        <div class="col">
            <div class="p-3 border">Column</div>
        </div>
        <div class="col">
            <div class="p-3 border">Column</div>
        </div>
        <div class="col">
            <div class="p-3 border">Column</div>
        </div>
    </div>

</div>

<div class="container mt-2">
```

```html
        <h2>Size 5 on x and y gutter</h2>

        <div class="row gx-5 gy-5">
            <div class="col">
                <div class="p-3 border">Column</div>
            </div>
            <div class="col">
                <div class="p-3 border">Column</div>
            </div>
            <div class="col">
                <div class="p-3 border">Column</div>
            </div>
            <div class="col">
                <div class="p-3 border">Column</div>
            </div>
            <div class="col">
                <div class="p-3 border">Column</div>
            </div>
            <div class="col">
                <div class="p-3 border">Column</div>
            </div>
            <div class="col">
                <div class="p-3 border">Column</div>
            </div>
            <div class="col">
                <div class="p-3 border">Column</div>
            </div>
            <div class="col">
                <div class="p-3 border">Column</div>
            </div>
            <div class="col">
                <div class="p-3 border">Column</div>
            </div>
        </div>

    </div>

    <script src="https://cdn.jsdelivr.net/npm/bootstrap@5.0.0-beta3/dist/js/bootstrap.bundle.min.js"></script>

</body>

</html>
```

NAV

The goal of the nav bar is to provide a branding image and some simple navigation elements that all neatly fold up into a large touchscreen-friendly burger menu.

The desktop version looks like this:

While the burger bar menu looks like this:

Home

Welcome

Container 1

Container 2

Container 3

The burger menu has a collapsed state as well.

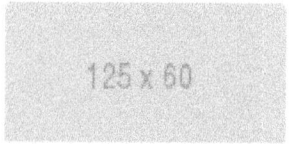

Always use the nav element when creating the top navigation bar. Assign it with the classes:

- navbar
- navbar-expanded
- navbar-light
- bg-light

Or

- navbar
- navbar-expanded-lg
- navbar-dark
- bg-dark

The first will produce a light bright navbar, while the second will present a dark one.

We can also use breakpoints, and I recommend adding -lg to the end of expanded.

The navbar class sets up all the formatting required for a navbar.

The navbar-expanded class allows the navbar to grow and shrink based on the window width. It allows that burger bar drop-down feature. The lg is a standard breakpoint, indicating when it should snap into mobile mode.

The navbar-light and navbar-dark classes simply set the text and background colours.

The basic class structure of a navbar looks like this:

- navbar navbar-expanded-lg navbar-light bg-light
    - container-fluid
        - navbar-brand
        - navbar-toggler
        - navbar-toggler-icon
        - collapse navbar-collapse
            - navbar-nav me-auto mb-2 mb-lg-0
                - nav-item
                    - nav-link active
                - nav-item
                    - nav-link

In addition to the classes we also have an ID `id="navbarSupportedContent"` and some data-bs-* attributes `data-bs-toggle="collapse"`

```html
1.  <nav class="navbar navbar-expand-lg navbar-light bg-light">
2.    <div class="container-fluid">
3.      <a class="navbar-brand" href="#"><img src="https://via.placeholder.com/125x60" class="card-img-top"
4.        alt="placeholder image"></a>
5.      <button class="navbar-toggler" type="button" data-bs-toggle="collapse" data-bs-target="#navbarSupportedContent">
6.        <span class="navbar-toggler-icon"></span>
7.      </button>
8.      <div class="collapse navbar-collapse" id="navbarSupportedContent">
9.        <ul class="navbar-nav me-auto mb-2 mb-lg-0">
10.         <li class="nav-item">
11.           <a class="nav-link active" aria-current="page" href="#">Home</a>
12.         </li>
13.         <li class="nav-item">
14.           <a class="nav-link" aria-current="page" href="#Welcome">Welcome</a>
15.         </li>
16.         <li class="nav-item">
17.           <a class="nav-link" aria-current="page" href="#Container1">Container 1</a>
18.         </li>
19.         <li class="nav-item">
20.           <a class="nav-link" aria-current="page" href="#Container2">Container 2</a>
21.         </li>
22.         <li class="nav-item">
23.           <a class="nav-link" aria-current="page" href="#Container3">Container 3</a>
24.         </li>
25.       </ul>
26.     </div>
27.   </div>
28. </nav>
```

These are used by the BootstrapJavaScript libraries and basically enable the interactive functionality. The data-bs stands for data Bootstrap, and as the name suggests it simply toggles states and provides targets for the code to interact with the elements.

This structure might look a little scary, but all you really have to do is copy and paste this block of code at the top of any website.

```html
1.  <nav class="navbar navbar-expand-lg navbar-light bg-light">
2.    <div class="container-fluid">
3.      <a class="navbar-brand" href="#"><img src="https://via.placeholder.com/125x60" class="card-img-top"
4.        alt="placeholder image"></a>
5.      <button class="navbar-toggler" type="button" data-bs-toggle="collapse" data-bs-target="#navbarSupportedContent">
6.        <span class="navbar-toggler-icon"></span>
7.      </button>
8.      <div class="collapse navbar-collapse" id="navbarSupportedContent">
9.        <ul class="navbar-nav me-auto mb-2 mb-lg-0">
10.         <li class="nav-item">
11.           <a class="nav-link active" aria-current="page" href="#">Home</a>
12.         </li>
13.         <li class="nav-item">
14.           <a class="nav-link" aria-current="page" href="#Welcome">Welcome</a>
15.         </li>
16.         <li class="nav-item">
17.           <a class="nav-link" aria-current="page" href="#Container1">Container 1</a>
18.         </li>
19.         <li class="nav-item">
20.           <a class="nav-link" aria-current="page" href="#Container2">Container 2</a>
21.         </li>
22.         <li class="nav-item">
23.           <a class="nav-link" aria-current="page" href="#Container3">Container 3</a>
24.         </li>
25.       </ul>
26.     </div>
27.   </div>
28. </nav>
```

The container-fluid can be swapped out for container and the branding, links and content will be centralised like a normal container.

The navbar-brand is where your brand image is placed. I recommend a small low-resolution image of around 125x60 or it will take up too much space.

A button is created with the navbar-toggler, which is a control that appears when the screen is thin enough and provides a styled button that drops the touch-friendly menu down.

The span inside navbar-toggler references the icon used. We use the default, but instead you could place an image or another icon class in here if you don't like the burger menu and prefer something like three dots.

The collapse navbar-collapse contains all the menu links you want to appear in your navbar. It is the target Bootstrap uses to swap between the item menu layout and the burger layout.

The navbar-nav and associated margin classes control how the items in the navbar are laid out.

Then we have the nav-item, which is where you place your links using a list structure format. Each navigation link must have nav-item as a class. The nav-link styles your <a> links into a navigation hyperlink. The active class indicates which page you are on. If you have a website with multiple places, and you are on a page other than home, the active class goes to that link item and gives a visual indication of where you are on the site.

- navbar navbar-expanded-lg navbar-light bg-light
    - container-fluid
        - navbar-brand
        - navbar-toggler
        - navbar-toggler-icon
        - collapse navbar-collapse
            - navbar-nav me-auto mb-2 mb-lg-0

- nav-item
  - nav-link active
- nav-item
  - nav-link

EXAMPLE 48
Below is a full example of a website, using navigation to move between multiple card groups.

```html
1.  <!doctype html>
2.  <html lang="en">
3.
4.  <head>
5.    <title>Navigation Bar</title>
6.    <meta charset="utf-8">
7.    <meta name="viewport" content="width=device-width, initial-scale=1">
8.    <link href="https://cdn.jsdelivr.net/npm/bootstrap@5.0.0-beta3/dist/css/bootstrap.min.css" rel="stylesheet">
9.  </head>
10.
11. <body>
12.
13.   <nav class="navbar navbar-expand-lg navbar-light bg-light">
14.     <div class="container-fluid">
15.       <a class="navbar-brand" href="#"><img src="https://via.placeholder.com/125x60" class="card-img-top"
16.           alt="placeholder image"></a>
17.       <button class="navbar-toggler" type="button" data-bs-toggle="collapse" data-bs-target="#navbarSupportedContent">
18.         <span class="navbar-toggler-icon"></span>
19.       </button>
20.       <div class="collapse navbar-collapse" id="navbarSupportedContent">
21.         <ul class="navbar-nav me-auto mb-2 mb-lg-0">
22.           <li class="nav-item">
23.             <a class="nav-link active" aria-current="page" href="#">Home</a>
24.           </li>
25.           <li class="nav-item">
26.             <a class="nav-link" aria-current="page" href="#Welcome">Welcome</a>
27.           </li>
28.           <li class="nav-item">
29.             <a class="nav-link" aria-current="page" href="#Container1">Container 1</a>
30.           </li>
31.           <li class="nav-item">
32.             <a class="nav-link" aria-current="page" href="#Container2">Container 2</a>
33.           </li>
34.           <li class="nav-item">
35.             <a class="nav-link" aria-current="page" href="#Container3">Container 3</a>
36.           </li>
37.         </ul>
38.       </div>
39.     </div>
40.   </nav>
41.
42.   <div class="container mt-2" id="Welcome">
43.     <div class="row">
44.       <div class="col-md-12 mb-2">
45.         <div class="card mb-3">
46.           <div class="row g-0">
47.             <div class="col-lg-4 d-none d-lg-block">
48.               <img src="https://via.placeholder.com/300x450" class="h-100" alt="null">
49.             </div>
50.             <div class="col-lg-8">
51.               <div class="card-body">
52.                 <h1 class="card-title">Footer</h1>
53.                 <p class="card-text">This is a demonstration of a footer in action.</p>
54.               </div>
55.             </div>
56.           </div>
57.         </div>
58.       </div>
59.     </div>
60.   </div>
61.
```

```
62.     <div class="container" id="Container1">
63.       <h2>Container 1</h2>
64.       <div class="row">
65.         <div class="col-md-6 mb-2">
66.           <div class="card">
67.             <img src="https://via.placeholder.com/350x150" class="card-img-top" alt="placeholder image">
68.             <div class="card-body">
69.               <h2 class="card-title">Card title</h2>
70.               <p class="card-text">Lorem ipsum dolor sit amet, consectetur adipiscing elit. Aliquam a semper urna.
71.                 Pellentesque at massa metus. Vivamus justo augue, accumsan sit amet odio ut, sollicitudin rhoncus leo.
72.                 Fusce non felis non mi fringilla tincidunt ac in arcu. Fusce elit justo, hendrerit eget augue a, suscipit
73.                 luctus urna. Aenean eu neque pulvinar, pharetra mauris at, facilisis est. Fusce eu commodo quam, eu
74.                 rhoncus tellus. Duis nec eros elit.</p>
75.               <a href="#" class="btn btn-primary">Go somewhere</a>
76.             </div>
77.             <div class="card-footer">
78.               Card footer
79.             </div>
80.           </div>
81.         </div>
82.         <div class="col-md-6 mb-2">
83.           <div class="card">
84.             <img src="https://via.placeholder.com/350x150" class="card-img-top" alt="placeholder image">
85.             <div class="card-body">
86.               <h2 class="card-title">Card title</h2>
87.               <p class="card-text">Lorem ipsum dolor sit amet, consectetur adipiscing elit. Aliquam a semper urna.
88.                 Pellentesque at massa metus. Vivamus justo augue, accumsan sit amet odio ut, sollicitudin rhoncus leo.
89.                 Fusce non felis non mi fringilla tincidunt ac in arcu. Fusce elit justo, hendrerit eget augue a, suscipit
90.                 luctus urna. Aenean eu neque pulvinar, pharetra mauris at, facilisis est. Fusce eu commodo quam, eu
91.                 rhoncus tellus. Duis nec eros elit.</p>
92.               <a href="#" class="btn btn-primary">Go somewhere</a>
93.             </div>
94.             <div class="card-footer">
95.               Card footer
96.             </div>
97.           </div>
98.         </div>
99.       </div>
100.    </div>
101.
102.    <div class="container" id="Container2">
103.      <h2>Cotnainer 2</h2>
104.      <div class="row">
105.        <div class="col-md-6 mb-2">
106.          <div class="card">
107.            <img src="https://via.placeholder.com/350x150" class="card-img-top" alt="placeholder image">
108.            <div class="card-body">
109.              <h2 class="card-title">Card title</h2>
110.              <p class="card-text">Lorem ipsum dolor sit amet, consectetur adipiscing elit. Aliquam a semper urna.
111.                Pellentesque at massa metus. Vivamus justo augue, accumsan sit amet odio ut, sollicitudin rhoncus leo.
112.                Fusce non felis non mi fringilla tincidunt ac in arcu. Fusce elit justo, hendrerit eget augue a, suscipit
113.                luctus urna. Aenean eu neque pulvinar, pharetra mauris at, facilisis est. Fusce eu commodo quam, eu
114.                rhoncus tellus. Duis nec eros elit.</p>
115.              <a href="#" class="btn btn-primary">Go somewhere</a>
116.            </div>
117.            <div class="card-footer">
```

```html
118.                Card footer
119.            </div>
120.        </div>
121.    </div>
122.    <div class="col-md-6 mb-2">
123.        <div class="card">
124.            <img src="https://via.placeholder.com/350x150" class="card-img-top" alt="placeholder image">
125.            <div class="card-body">
126.                <h2 class="card-title">Card title</h2>
127.                <p class="card-text">Lorem ipsum dolor sit amet, consectetur adipiscing elit. Aliquam a semper urna.
128.                Pellentesque at massa metus. Vivamus justo augue, accumsan sit amet odio ut, sollicitudin rhoncus leo.
129.                Fusce non felis non mi fringilla tincidunt ac in arcu. Fusce elit justo, hendrerit eget augue a, suscipit
130.                luctus urna. Aenean eu neque pulvinar, pharetra mauris at, facilisis est. Fusce eu commodo quam, eu
131.                rhoncus tellus. Duis nec eros elit.</p>
132.                <a href="#" class="btn btn-primary">Go somewhere</a>
133.            </div>
134.            <div class="card-footer">
135.                Card footer
136.            </div>
137.        </div>
138.    </div>
139.    </div>
140. </div>
141.
142. <div class="container" id="Container3">
143.    <h2>Cotnainer 3</h2>
144.    <div class="row">
145.        <div class="col-md-6 mb-2">
146.            <div class="card">
147.                <img src="https://via.placeholder.com/350x150" class="card-img-top" alt="placeholder image">
148.                <div class="card-body">
149.                    <h2 class="card-title">Card title</h2>
150.                    <p class="card-text">Lorem ipsum dolor sit amet, consectetur adipiscing elit. Aliquam a semper urna.
151.                    Pellentesque at massa metus. Vivamus justo augue, accumsan sit amet odio ut, sollicitudin rhoncus leo.
152.                    Fusce non felis non mi fringilla tincidunt ac in arcu. Fusce elit justo, hendrerit eget augue a, suscipit
153.                    luctus urna. Aenean eu neque pulvinar, pharetra mauris at, facilisis est. Fusce eu commodo quam, eu
154.                    rhoncus tellus. Duis nec eros elit.</p>
155.                <a href="#" class="btn btn-primary">Go somewhere</a>
156.            </div>
157.            <div class="card-footer">
158.                Card footer
159.            </div>
160.        </div>
161.    </div>
162.    <div class="col-md-6 mb-2">
163.        <div class="card">
164.            <img src="https://via.placeholder.com/350x150" class="card-img-top" alt="placeholder image">
165.            <div class="card-body">
166.                <h2 class="card-title">Card title</h2>
167.                <p class="card-text">Lorem ipsum dolor sit amet, consectetur adipiscing elit. Aliquam a semper urna.
168.                Pellentesque at massa metus. Vivamus justo augue, accumsan sit amet odio ut, sollicitudin rhoncus leo.
169.                Fusce non felis non mi fringilla tincidunt ac in arcu. Fusce elit justo, hendrerit eget augue a, suscipit
170.                luctus urna. Aenean eu neque pulvinar, pharetra mauris at, facilisis est. Fusce eu commodo quam, eu
171.                rhoncus tellus. Duis nec eros elit.</p>
172.                <a href="#" class="btn btn-primary">Go somewhere</a>
173.            </div>
```

```
174.            <div class="card-footer">
175.                Card footer
176.            </div>
177.          </div>
178.        </div>
179.      </div>
180.    </div>
181.
182.    <script src="https://cdn.jsdelivr.net/npm/bootstrap@5.0.0-beta3/dist/js/bootstrap.bundle.min.js">
183.    </script>
184.
185. </body>
186.
187. </html>
```

FOOTER

The footer serves as the place to store your copyright information, navigation links and some parting words for those who have reached the end of the page.

A standard Bootstrap footer looks like this:

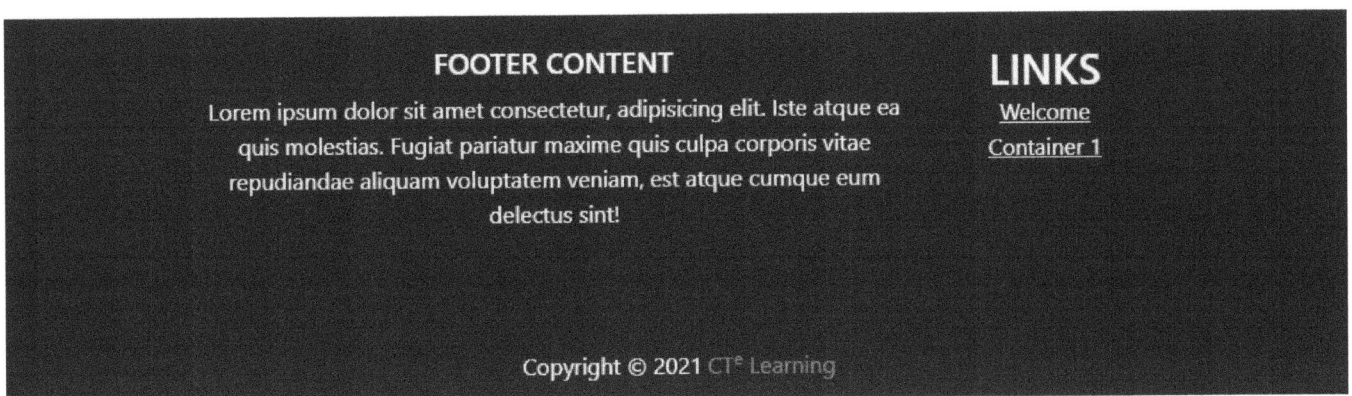

It is achieved using the footer div as well as some simple colour styling and text effects.

A single container is used, along with a row and a couple of columns. These make up the content and hyperlinks.

Below that we place a simple div with some centred text.

The standard code for a footer looks like this:

```
1.    <footer class="bg-dark text-light text-center text-lg-start">
2.      <div class="container p-4">
3.        <div class="row">
4.          <div class="col-md-9 mb-4">
5.            <h5 class="text-uppercase">Footer Content</h5>
6.            <p> Lorem ipsum dolor sit amet consectetur, adipisicing elit. Iste atque ea quis molestias. Fugiat pariatur maxime quis culpa corporis vitae repudiandae aliquam voluptatem veniam, est atque cumque eum delectus sint! </p>
7.          </div>
8.
9.          <div class="col-md-3 mb-4">
10.           <h2 class="text-uppercase mb-0">Links</h5>
11.           <ul class="list-unstyled">
12.             <li><a href="#Welcome" class="text-light">Welcome</a></li>
13.             <li><a href="#Container1" class="text-light">Container 1</a></li>
```

```
14.                </ul>
15.             </div>
16.         </div>
17.     </div>
18.
19.     <div class="text-center p-3">Copyright © 2021 <a class="text-primary text-decoration-none" href="https://www.ctelearning.com">CT<sup>e</sup> Learning</a>
20.     </div>
21.
22. </footer>
23.
```

You can copy and paste it to the end of any document, then make only minimal changes.

EXAMPLE 49

```html
1.  <!doctype html>
2.  <html lang="en">
3.
4.  <head>
5.      <title>Footer</title>
6.      <meta charset="utf-8">
7.      <meta name="viewport" content="width=device-width, initial-scale=1">
8.      <link href="https://cdn.jsdelivr.net/npm/bootstrap@5.0.0-beta3/dist/css/bootstrap.min.css" rel="stylesheet"
9.          >
10. </head>
11.
12. <body>
13.
14.     <nav class="navbar navbar-expand-lg navbar-light bg-light">
15.         <div class="container-fluid">
16.             <a class="navbar-brand" href="#"><img src="https://via.placeholder.com/125x60" class="card-img-top"
17.                     alt="placeholder image"></a>
18.             <button class="navbar-toggler" type="button" data-bs-toggle="collapse"
19.                 data-bs-target="#navbarSupportedContent" aria-controls="navbarSupportedContent" aria-expanded="false"
20.                 aria-label="Toggle navigation">
21.                 <span class="navbar-toggler-icon"></span>
22.             </button>
23.             <div class="collapse navbar-collapse" id="navbarSupportedContent">
24.                 <ul class="navbar-nav me-auto mb-2 mb-lg-0">
25.                     <li class="nav-item">
26.                         <a class="nav-link active" aria-current="page" href="#">Home</a>
27.                     </li>
28.                     <li class="nav-item dropdown">
29.                         <a class="nav-link dropdown-toggle" href="#" id="navbarDropdown" role="button"
30.                             data-bs-toggle="dropdown" aria-expanded="false">
31.                             Dropdown menu
32.                         </a>
33.                         <ul class="dropdown-menu" aria-labelledby="navbarDropdown">
34.                             <li><a class="dropdown-item" href="#Welcome">Welcome</a></li>
35.                             <li><a class="dropdown-item" href="#Container1">Container 1</a></li>
36.                         </ul>
37.                     </li>
38.                 </ul>
39.             </div>
40.         </div>
41.     </nav>
42.
43.     <div class="container mt-2" id="Welcome">
44.         <div class="row">
45.             <div class="col-md-12 mb-2">
46.                 <div class="card mb-3">
47.                     <div class="row g-0">
48.                         <div class="col-md-4">
49.                             <img src="https://via.placeholder.com/300x450" class="h-100" alt="null">
50.                         </div>
51.                         <div class="col-md-8">
52.                             <div class="card-body">
53.                                 <h1 class="card-title">Footer</h1>
54.                                 <p class="card-text">This is a demonstration of a footer in action.</p>
55.                             </div>
56.                         </div>
57.                     </div>
58.                 </div>
59.             </div>
60.         </div>
61.     </div>
62.
63.     <div class="container" id="Container1">
```

```
64.            <h2>Container 1</h2>
65.            <div class="row">
66.                <div class="col-md-6 mb-2">
67.                    <div class="card">
68.                        <img src="https://via.placeholder.com/350x150" class="card-img-top" alt="placeholder image">
69.                        <div class="card-body">
70.                            <h2 class="card-title">Card title</h2>
71.                            <p class="card-text">Lorem ipsum dolor sit amet, consectetur adipiscing elit. Aliquam a semper
72.                                urna.
73.                                Pellentesque at massa metus. Vivamus justo augue, accumsan sit amet odio ut, sollicitudin
74.                                rhoncus leo.
75.                                Fusce non felis non mi fringilla tincidunt ac in arcu. Fusce elit justo, hendrerit eget
76.                                augue a, suscipit
77.                                luctus urna. Aenean eu neque pulvinar, pharetra mauris at, facilisis est. Fusce eu commodo
78.                                quam, eu
79.                                rhoncus tellus. Duis nec eros elit.</p>
80.                            <a href="#" class="btn btn-primary">Go somewhere</a>
81.                        </div>
82.                        <div class="card-footer">
83.                            Card footer
84.                        </div>
85.                    </div>
86.                </div>
87.                <div class="col-md-6 mb-2">
88.                    <div class="card">
89.                        <img src="https://via.placeholder.com/350x150" class="card-img-top" alt="placeholder image">
90.                        <div class="card-body">
91.                            <h2 class="card-title">Card title</h2>
92.                            <p class="card-text">Lorem ipsum dolor sit amet, consectetur adipiscing elit. Aliquam a semper
93.                                urna.
94.                                Pellentesque at massa metus. Vivamus justo augue, accumsan sit amet odio ut, sollicitudin
95.                                rhoncus leo.
96.                                Fusce non felis non mi fringilla tincidunt ac in arcu. Fusce elit justo, hendrerit eget
97.                                augue a, suscipit
98.                                luctus urna. Aenean eu neque pulvinar, pharetra mauris at, facilisis est. Fusce eu commodo
99.                                quam, eu
100.                                rhoncus tellus. Duis nec eros elit.</p>
101.                            <a href="#" class="btn btn-primary">Go somewhere</a>
102.                        </div>
103.                        <div class="card-footer">
104.                            Card footer
105.                        </div>
106.                    </div>
107.                </div>
108.            </div>
109.        </div>
110.
111.        <footer class="bg-dark text-light text-center text-lg-start">
112.            <div class="container p-4">
113.                <div class="row">
114.                    <div class="col-md-9 mb-4">
115.                        <h5 class="text-uppercase">Footer Content</h5>
116.                        <p> Lorem ipsum dolor sit amet consectetur, adipisicing elit. Iste atque ea quis molestias. Fugiat pariatur maxime quis culpa corporis vitae repudiandae aliquam voluptatem veniam, est atque cumque eum delectus sint! </p>
117.                    </div>
118.
119.                    <div class="col-md-3 mb-4">
```

```html
120.                        <h2 class="text-uppercase mb-0">Links</h5>
121.                        <ul class="list-unstyled">
122.                            <li><a href="#Welcome" class="text-light">Welcome</a></li>
123.                            <li><a href="#Container1" class="text-light">Container 1</a></li>
124.                        </ul>
125.                    </div>
126.                </div>
127.            </div>
128.
129.            <div class="text-center p-3">Copyright © 2021 <a class="text-primary text-decoration-none" href="https://www.ctelearning.com">CT<sup>e</sup> Learning</a>
130.            </div>
131.
132.        </footer>
133.
134.
135.        <script src="https://cdn.jsdelivr.net/npm/bootstrap@5.0.0-beta3/dist/js/bootstrap.bundle.min.js">
136.        </script>
137.
138.    </body>
139.
140. </html>
```

END OF SECTION ACTIVITY

You've learned everything you need to create a fully featured website with navigation, content, and a footer. You should practice your skills and make a multipage website. Look at other sites on the web and see if you can recreate them using bootstrap. Look at mobile sites and see how they work and how well bootstrap compares.

Sit down and imagine what direction you want to take your new skills in. Are you going to design a website for yourself or are you going to jump into Fiverr and start promoting your skills for jobs.

No matter what you do, the next step has to be "making a portfolio". A portfolio is a tool you can fall back on when attempting to get work, or demonstrating to clients why they want to hire you.

Practice making lots of websites, using all kinds of layouts.

It will help get you work, jobs and develop your skills further.

It will also help you identify where you are lacking in your skills or understanding.

THE NEXT STEP IN YOUR CAREER

You now know the technical knowledge you need to produce good quality bootstrap websites. The next step should be to practice your new skills. I would strongly recommend producing your own portfolio if you seek work, online jobs, and others. Books are a great starting point, but it can never replace hands on experience.

To help support your future career, I've partnered with **CT· Learning** a number of courses will support the bootstrap foundations chapters you've just completed you can find a list of these courses at https://www.ctelearning.com/b5f

This book was written with the support of https://www.ctelearning.com for all your career and technical education needs.

CT^eLearning.com
Powered by I Support Learning, Inc.

INDEX

.display-1, 38
.display-6, 38
1140px, 87
1320px, 87
720px, 87
960px, 87
About, 10
align text, 47
Bootstrap headings, 29
Bootstrap versions, 15
border, 68, 70
border-1, 70
border-2, 70
border-3, 70
border-4, 70
border-5, 70
border-bottom, 68
border-danger, 68
border-dark, 68
border-end, 68
border-info, 68
border-light, 68
border-primary, 68
border-secondary, 68
border-start, 68
border-success, 68
border-top, 68
border-warning, 68
breakpoint, 97
breakpoints, 102
btn class, 78
btn-danger, 78
btn-dark, 78
btn-info, 78
btn-light, 78
btn-primary, 78
btn-secondary, 78
btn-success, 78
btn-warning, 78
buttons, 78, 82
Buttons, 78, 81
Cards, 108
Center Align, 47
class *col*, 94
col class, 98
col-lg-*, 103
col-md-*, 103
Colours, 65
col-sm-*, 103
column, 102
columns, 105
Columns, 96

col-xl-*, 103
col-xxl-*, 103
container-fluid, 90
container-lg, 88
container-md, 88
containers, 86
container-sm, 88
container-xl, 88
container-xxl, 88
create a row, 93
CSS class system, 23
Danger, 65
Dark, 65
Display headings, 38
display-1, 38, 41
display-2, 41
End Align, 47
evenly distribute the space between the columns, 98
float-end, 106
float-start, 106
font sizes, 51
Font Sizing, 51
footer, 131
front-end web, 11
fs-1, 51
fs-2, 51
fs-3, 51
fs-4, 51
fs-5, 51
fs-6, 51
fst-italic, 54
fst-normal, 54
fw-bold, 54
fw-bolder, 54
fw-light, 54
fw-lighter, 54
fw-normal, 54
Getting Started, 18
grid system, 92
group buttons, 80
Gutters, 115
gx-*, 115, 116, 121
gy-*, 115, 118, 121
h1, 26, 30, 31
h6, 26, 31
Headings Typography, 26
horizontal gutter sizing, 116
Images, 106
img-fluid, 106
img-thumbnail, 106
Info, 65
lead text, 44

Lead Text, 43
leading texts, 44
Light, 65
Line height, 57
Lists, 63
list-unstyled, 63
m-*, 73, 77
m-1, 71
m-2, 71
m-3, 71
m-4, 71
m-5, 71
margin, 73
margins, 72
Margins, 71
mb-*, 73, 77
me-*, 73, 77
ms-*, 73, 77
mt-*, 73, 77
multiple rows, 99
mx-*, 73, 77
mx-auto, 106
my-*, 73, 77
nav bar, 124
navigation, 128
normal text, 61
Outline buttons, 81
p-1, 75
p-2, 75
p-3, 75
p-4, 75
p-5, 75
padding, 76
Padding, 75
pair of cards, 113
Primary, 65
removal of underline, 61
Requirements, 13

Responsive Layout, 85
row of content, 93
Search Engine Optimization, 34
Secondary, 65
Secondary heading, 35
SEO, 34
sizes of text, 52
Start Align, 47
~~straight through text~~, 61
STRIKE, 61
strikethrough, 61
Success, 65
Text Alignment, 47
Text Line-height, 57
Text Transform, 59
text-capitalise, 59, 60
text-center, 47, 48
text-decoration-line-through, 62
text-decoration-none, 62
text-decoration-underline, 62
text-end, 47, 48
text-lowercase, 59, 60
text-start, 47, 48
text-uppercase, 59, 60
Typography, 25
underline, 61
Underline, 61
underlined text, 62
unstyled class, 63
unstyled list, 64
w-100, 106
w-25, 106
w-50, 106
w-75, 106
Warning, 65
weight, 54
What is Bootstrap?, 14
What's new, 17

www.ingramcontent.com/pod-product-compliance
Ingram Content Group UK Ltd.
Pitfield, Milton Keynes, MK11 3LW, UK
UKHW050414240426
12048UKWH00020B/1506